Briefly:
Nietzsche's *Beyond Good and Evil*

The SCM *Briefly* series

Briefly: Nietzsche's
Beyond Good and Evil

David Mills Daniel
and
Dafydd Mills Daniel

scm press

The authors and publisher acknowledge material reproduced from
Friedrich Nietzsche, *Beyond Good and Evil*, translated by Marion Faber,
Oxford and New York: Oxford University Press, 1998, ISBN 0192832638.
Reproduced by permission of Oxford University Press.
All rights reserved.

British Library Cataloguing in Publication data

A catalogue record for this book is available
from the British Library

978 0 334 04123 8

First published in 2007 by SCM Press
13–17 Long Lane,
London ECIA 9PN

www.scm-canterburypress.co.uk

SCM Press is a division of
SCM-Canterbury Press Ltd

Typeset by Regent Typesetting, London
Printed and bound in Great Britain by
CPI Bookmarque, Croydon, Surrey

Contents

Introduction

The SCM *Briefly* series, edited by David Mills Daniel, is designed to enable students and general readers to acquire knowledge and understanding of key texts in philosophy, philosophy of religion, theology and ethics. While the series will be especially helpful to those following university and A-level courses in philosophy, ethics and religious studies, it will in fact be of interest to anyone looking for a short guide to the ideas of a particular philosopher or theologian.

Each book in the series takes a piece of work by one philosopher and provides a summary of the original text, which adheres closely to it, and contains direct quotations from it, thus enabling the reader to follow each development in the philosopher's argument(s). Throughout the summary, there are page references to the original philosophical writing, so that the reader has ready access to the primary text. In the Introduction to each book, you will find details of the edition of the philosophical work referred to.

In *Briefly: Nietzsche's Beyond Good and Evil*, we refer to Friedrich Nietzsche, *Beyond Good and Evil*, translated by Marion Faber, Oxford and New York: Oxford University Press, 1998, ISBN 0192832638.

Each *Briefly* begins with an Introduction, followed by a chapter on the Context in which the work was written. Who was this writer? Why was this book written? With Some Issues to Consider, and some Suggestions for Further Reading, this *Briefly* aims to get anyone started in their philosophical investigation. The Detailed Summary of the philosophical work is followed by a concise chapter-by-chapter Overview and an extensive Glossary of terms.

Bold type is used in the Detailed Summary and Overview sections to indicate the first occurrence of words and phrases that appear in the Glossary. The Glossary also contains terms used elsewhere in this *Briefly* guide and other terms that readers may encounter in their study of Nietzsche's *Beyond Good and Evil*.

Context

Who was Friedrich Nietzsche?

Friedrich Wilhelm Nietzsche was born at Röcken bei Lutzen, near Leipzig, Germany, in 1844. His father, a Lutheran minister, died in 1849, and Nietzsche's mother moved the family to Naumburg, where they received a strict religious upbringing. After being a scholar at Schulpforta boarding school, Nietzsche entered Bonn University in 1864, but transferred to Leipzig University a year later, remaining there (apart from a year's military service in 1867) until 1868. At Leipzig he dropped the study of theology, but maintained his interest in philology. He developed an enthusiasm for the work of Schopenhauer and Wagner, whom he would later view as philosophical opponents.

From 1869, Nietzsche taught classical philology at Basle University, Switzerland, where he was appointed to a full professorship in 1870. His first book, *The Birth of Tragedy out of the Spirit of Music*, was published in 1872, and received some negative attention. His other works include *Human, All Too Human: A Book for Free Spirits* (1878), *Thus Spake Zarathustra: A Book for Everyone and No One* (1883–85), *On the Genealogy of Morals: A Polemic* (1887), *Twilight of the Idols, or How to*

Philosophize with a Hammer (1889), and *The Antichrist: Curse on Christianity* (1895).

Nietzsche suffered a complete mental collapse in 1889 and was committed to an asylum. After his discharge in 1890, he was cared for by his mother, until her death in 1897, and then by his sister. Nietzsche died in 1900.

What is *Beyond Good and Evil?*

Beyond Good and Evil: Prelude to a Philosophy of the Future was first published in 1886, and is one of the most interesting and popular of Nietzsche's works, dealing with many themes that are characteristic of his philosophy. The Sections covered in this *Briefly* (1–3, 5, 6, 9) take us through (among other things) Nietzsche's theories of the will to truth and to power; the perverseness of Christianity; master and slave morality; and the 'new', or 'true', philosopher.

Beyond Good and Evil is written in an aphoristic style, and Nietzsche guides us, in a disjointed way, through a history of human ideas and emotions, and their expression in philosophy, religion and society. However, definite themes run through each section of aphorisms, and these connect and build through the work as a whole, leading the reader, if not to a definite and clearly expressed conclusion, then to an inexpressible feeling of uncertainty. Throughout our reading of the book, we have the impression of beginning to understand his arguments, yet, in some sense, not fully grasping his philosophy. Nietzsche seems to want us to trust his view of the world, but also to be uncertain and wary of it. For Nietzsche, this tension in his reader between certainty and uncertainty would mean that the force of his truth has been felt as something that is difficult to accept, but impossible to ignore, once revealed. Also, a tension between scepticism and acceptance is the effect Nietzsche wants his philosophy to have on our conceptual understandings of such ideological constructs as 'humanity' and 'world', and the way we have formularized and responded to them in various philosophical systems and religions. He encourages us to doubt, and then to doubt even the validity of our doubting, before we move 'beyond' with him.

In Sections 2 and 3, Nietzsche argues against philosophical and religious dogmatism. He refers to sceptical free spirits, and the way that France demonstrated cultural dominance over Europe, in his time, by teaching and displaying the 'glamour of scepticism'; thus, he appears to endorse the need for it. However, he often regards scepticism as being as undesirable as dogmatism, particularly religious dogmatism. Scepticism demonstrates an animosity towards the spirit and the human will, analogous to that in, for example, Christianity and Buddhism (see also Section 5). In his view, Christianity counteracts the spirit by seeking to confine it, making it seek its own denial, as though that which contradicts the spirit is its essential meaning. Christianity makes desire, in accordance with the true, active vitality of the spirit, sinful, and instead promotes isolation, asceticism and restraint. Similarly, scepticism, with its emphasis on being non-committal and using intellect to contain impulse, contradicts and perverts what should be the spirit's essential, instinctual vitality and dynamism.

Thus, as we might expect, there are certain ironies and paradoxes in Nietzsche's thought. For example, the 'new' philosophers (Section 6) must be capable of a view 'downwards'. This is a panoramic vision of the whole of life and human existence, in which, and through which, the philosopher goes beyond good and evil and the timid norms of received social

3

and religious morality. But the true philosopher, as well as being 'above', must also be involved. The new philosophers cannot, and will not, conform to the 'rabble's' stereotypical view of the philosophical life, as a means of escaping the world's puzzles and trials: the 'wicked game'. They are not detached, or set apart from life, but live unphilosophically and unwisely, enduring the burdensome duty of a hundred of life's tests and temptations.

Again, Nietzsche's understanding of 'spirit' and 'spirituality' (Section 3) gives us pause for thought. His view that Christian doctrine amounts to a perversion of the will and spirit does not mean that the Christian saint has no will, but that it is a perverse one: it is the will to denial. The saint's recognition that his will to power is satisfied in the repression of spirit, which shows his strength in self-containment, is a shocking display of a religious neurosis that is obsessive and gratuitous; and, in the way that it resists and condemns desires that are natural to human beings, criminal. So, if it is not to be found in the saintly and hermit-like existence of contemplative ascetics, who have disengaged from worldliness, what is 'spirituality' or the spiritual life for Nietzsche? It is the true, raw strength to live life as life, in a way that embodies the complex and frightening truths and absurdities of existence, from which we often try to escape, as they are too much for us. Spirituality is living with life always in sight, and coming to terms with, and freely living out, its unpredictability, unfairness and vibrancy. The attempt to conceal life's absurdities and inequalities, by imposing such artificial contrivances as the neat distinction between good and evil on to it, is to hide from life, and to diminish its value and variety, cheapening it and making it into what it is not. By the use of paradox and irony, he aims to deconstruct certain aspects of human existence. In doing so, he implicitly, and sometimes (in a dramatic way) explicitly, constructs the means by which human beings might begin to recognize what, for him, lies at the heart of an authentic human existence: release into the freedom to exist truly and magnificently as a collection of individuals, who are honest with themselves and the world. Obviously, such a complex process has a number of stages and elements.

To start with (Section I), we must examine critically our obsession with truth. Philosophers and theologians all want to find and reveal the truth, and we all want to hear them, because we want to know what it is. The problem is that we should actually be questioning the value of our will to truth and what philosophers and theologians proclaim to us as truth. One of Nietzsche's greatest insights is that most conscious thinking has to be considered as an 'instinctual' activity. There is nothing dry, detached, or truly objective about any argument, no matter how much it is dressed up in dispassionate rationality or complex philosophical logic. Value judgements lie behind everything, and these are biases that lead thinkers, in their will to truth, to will one that confirms their particular prejudices. They have become instinctive, because they are seen as undeniable, and are automatically and unthinkingly affirmed. Nietzsche wants us to question the validity of these seemingly self-evident value judgements. Uncritically, we suppose that certainty is worth more than uncertainty, or appearance less than truth, but why? Nietzsche is critical of Kant (Section I) for enquiring about the possibility of synthetic *a priori* judgements. The answer is irrelevant; the real question concerns why belief in them is necessary. For Nietzsche, it is because they have regulatory importance: we would like them to be true, and find it impossible to live happily and peacefully in a world where we cannot imagine our (moral) values to be the fundamental truths of existence. However, our view that, for example, truth is more valuable than falsity could be no more than a 'foreground evaluation'. We need to believe in the truth of such judgements, as they serve to preserve creatures like us, but they could be false.

This does not mean that our false judgements, and 'logical fictions', have no value: indeed, to give them up would be to deny life. It is just that regarding our value judgements as truth prevents us from seeing life as it really is, and recognizing our truths and value judgements for what they really are: untruths, necessary to the way we want to see life, but which bear no relation to what it really is. The new philosophers will appreciate that there is no point in objecting to a judgement, just because it is false. They will come to terms with the fact that false judgements are the most fundamental to life; and, in admitting untruth as a condition of life, will place themselves beyond good and evil, as they free themselves from the distinctions we make, as a result of our judgements, not as a result of the true nature of existence.

Past philosophers have failed to engage with the complexity of existence, and to be honest with themselves. The Stoics (Section 1) pretended to themselves and the world that they understood the truth, because they had learned it from Nature. However, they had simply imposed their own image on to Nature, and made life appear as they wanted it to appear, by making the world conform to their own values. As a result, they cheated themselves, by believing that what they projected on to Nature was the truth, and they cheapened existence by making it easier to understand. By ignoring its unfathomable mystery and complexity, and ordering it under a system of untruth, they turned Nature into something they could profess to understand. Descartes (Sections 3 and 5), all subsequent philosophers who had dealt sympathetically with his 'I Think [therefore I am]', and Schopenhauer (Sections 1, 2, 3, 5 and 6), with his 'I Will [therefore I am]', had done no better. Like the 'common people', they assumed that there could be such 'immediate certainties'. The philosopher should realize that nothing is revealed or explained by his saying that he can be certain he exists because thinking or willing exists. Thinking and willing are far more complicated than that. The proposition 'I think' involves a series of metaphysical questions, which cannot be satisfactorily answered: for example, that the 'I' is the one thinking; that there has to be a something doing the thinking; that an 'I' exists; and that it is known what thinking is. Further, although 'will' and 'think' are single words, this does not mean that they can be straightforwardly explained: willing is complicated, and only has unity as a word.

Human beings seek to simplify everything, and, as a result, make existence less difficult, and so less magnificent than it is. We try to comfort ourselves with fictions, in order to resolve life's complexities into an order that appeals to our lack of imagination and desire for things to be easy. But, in the end, we must accept the fact that we have not explained anything. Physics (Section 1) appeals to our 'plebeian' tastes, because it involves belief in something we can see or touch; but even physics has a perspective, a prejudiced and particular point of view, and so is only a way of interpreting or arranging the world. It is the same with cause and effect, freedom of the will, determinism, reason, purpose, and so on. They are all concepts that we have invented, which should be treated as conventional fictions, for the purpose of description and communication, not as explanations. The problem is that we read our concepts into life itself, and so they prevent us from looking at how things might be without them, which could be how things really are. The systems of thinking we have devised interfere with our understanding of life, and make it difficult for us to appreciate it fully, and to live properly. For example, life does not really throw up the question of whether the will is or is not free: in real life, it is only a matter of wills that are strong or weak.

The new philosophers will engage with life, and place themselves beyond good and evil, by realizing that even such ideals as the opposition of values and democratic justice are merely our false judgements, imposed on the world, which artificially constrain it, and make it easier for the weakest among us to survive, if not succeed. The new philosopher will see that, just as the idea that truth is preferable to falsity is a value judgement, so is the idea that evil cannot come out of good. He will question whether such values as good and evil really are opposites; whether, in fact, they even exist. For Nietzsche, part of the problem with past thinkers has been that they have taken morality as a given. He wants us to enter a new world of dangerous insights, turning the apparently positive values of religion and morality on their head, and thereby cancelling out the negative influence of Plato, who, through his invention of pure spirit and transcendental goodness (in his theory of the forms), originally set truth on its head. Plato's ideas (Preface, Sections 1 and 5) have led human beings to look for meaning beyond themselves, beyond their bodies and the material world. Plato's influence has led to a devaluation of physical life, and given us the fiction of something more understandable and worthwhile than the confusion of the human world, with all its variety and complexity. Plato invented the ideal of the Good and the separate spiritual kingdom, and made them more powerful and important than this world, by saying that whatever is not material is superior.

The Christian religion (Section 3), by propagating such myths, has mutated the natural order, and caused confusion and distress in the hearts of those human beings who want to feel their worth in a world where they can be physically active, rather than spiritually castrated. For Christianity, following Plato, has made what is weak and soft into what is good, and made it impossible to grasp the physical world through exuberant and fulfilling activity. Thus, it not only teaches that there is sin, but that suffering is holy, and (worst of all) that those who suffer most are the most holy, and superior even to those who are noble and naturally powerful. Through its propagation of solitude, fasting and sexual abstinence, it is world-denying. The saint embodies a 'monstrous' denial, which is contrary to nature, and he is joined by others who are perversely prepared to sacrifice, to God, the strongest instincts they possess. Christianity perverts and confuses the will to power, by making it seek power in its own contradiction: a power through lack of power, triumph through debasement.

Plato, the Stoics and the saint have, in many ways, found their will to power satisfied in their will to truth: they have all managed to project their own image on to the whole of existence, and made acceptance of their truth necessary to a proper understanding of life and to success in it. When we look at someone like a saint, we cannot but wonder if there is anything in what he professes, whether such an extreme sacrifice means that there really is some mighty power elsewhere, which the saint knows about and we do not. Thus, it is the saint's perverted will to power that causes him to accept the Christian message, and to behave in the way that he does, while it is also the will to power that brings us, in our fear of what lies behind such an ignoble and revolting pathological denial of the world and oneself, to acknowledge him.

9

According to Nietzsche, the interest that the Christian saint engenders has had obscene consequences. Nietzsche (Section 9) endorses an aristocratic hierarchy, where those at the top are there by nature. They are effortlessly noble and intrinsically superior to those beneath them. They do not need to think about who and what they are, or what is right or wrong: they just are, and need no further guidance in, or explanation of, truth, morality or existence, apart from themselves. Their superiority reflects the naturalness of their instinct just to be, and, by being, to exist powerfully and above others, without considering anything other than their impulses. Nietzsche's ideal man (his ideal could only be masculine) is thus reminiscent of George Bernard Shaw's understanding of Julius Caesar: '... in order to produce an impression of complete disinterestedness and magnanimity, he has only to act with entire selfishness; and this is perhaps the only sense in which a man can be said to be *naturally* great ... Having virtue, he has no need of goodness. He is neither forgiving, frank, nor generous, because a man who is too great to resent has nothing to forgive.'

Plato and Christianity, by separating power, nobility and truth from activity and physicality, have upset the natural order. In their petty morality, which venerates weakness, self-sacrifice and pity, rather than noble human dignity and self-sufficiency, they have exploited an untruth, by making spirituality something that can be isolated from physical magnificence. As a result, those who should be slaves can be masters.

Nietzsche (Section 3) holds that there are necessarily suffering individuals and failed cases: the deformed, sick, degenerating and frail. Ideally, religion should comfort them, reconciling them to their role of existing only to serve and be generally useful, and encouraging them to be even more obedient and subservient. By justifying the baseness and semi-animal poverty of their souls, religion can pretend that their lowliness and suffering means something, thus making them not only content with their inferiority, but willing to accept further degradation, which, they think, raises them within an illusory higher order of things. They are then satisfied to remain in their rightful place (at the bottom) in the real order.

The problem is that religions like Christianity and Buddhism have idealized suffering. In consequence, they have not only contributed to the European race's degeneration, by assisting the survival of the sick and suffering, thus unnaturally preserving the weakest individuals, whose short lives are meant only for service, but also turned all values upside down. It is now the weak and suffering, the so-called spiritual people, who are viewed as the best and most worthy, not the powerful and strong, who, by nature, are really the most significant, and who should rule over the rest. With the misguided belief that all are equal in God's eyes, Christianity has criminalized the instincts of the highest and best-formed species of human beings, the autocratic, masculine, triumphant and tyrannical, and designated pity, renunciation and forgiveness as holy. These are the instincts of the weak, who are unable to claim recognition for themselves in this world by physical means, but who convince us that there is another world, more important than this one, which they will rule.

Nietzsche has no patience for the ideals of democratic justice (Sections 5 and 9), regarding it as another example of the human failure to engage truly with reality, in all its terrifying and glorious complexity. Increasingly, human beings are insufficiently noble, strong or far-sighted to accept the gulf between human and human, and to think about what this means, when philosophizing about the purpose and nature of humanity and the world. While neither high-minded nor tough enough to grasp the nature of existence, with our value judgements and logical fictions, we still arrogantly presume that we can understand existence, and, like the Stoics, even seek to determine the meaning and value of life, according to our own preferences and contrary to how it really is. Christianity, with its world-denying aspects, such as the precedence it gives to meekness, asceticism and equality, has been the most dangerous form of human presumption.

Thus, Nietzsche (Sections 5 and 6) challenges Enlightenment philosophy, which, adapting the Christian belief in all being equal before God, promulgated the idea that everyone is entitled to the same equal and fair treatment. But, if everyone is equal, and must be taken account of and treated fairly, no matter how weak or lowly, the human animal cannot rise above the mediocre. Anything that stands out, which is individual and vital, comes to be seen as dangerous, resulting in a struggle against everything that glorifies the best of human life: the privileged, the higher human, the higher soul. Now that the entire human 'herd' must be taken into account, the desires and demands of the weak and desperate are just as important as those of the strong, such as the new philosophers, who should be ruling over them. In fact, through the Christian reversal of what is spiritually important and significant, the demands of the weak and the oppressed take precedence, because, according to Christian teaching, it is, perversely, the weakest individuals who are the most spiritual and thus powerful. As a result, the community of the herd matters more than the individual, because the herd will give priority to the community, as they can only survive in a community of equality and pity. The peace and comfort of the weak depends upon a society that is mediocre and valueless, because, in the softness of their will, the weak fear the original, dramatic and powerful. The herd community, which seeks to protect everyone from fear and suffering, and promotes the weak, is threatened whenever an individual's highest and strongest instincts break forth with passion, and drives him above the average. So, everything that elevates the individual instils fear in the community, and is regarded as evil. Through Christianity, the weak have been able to promote compassion and pity as the highest goods, and doing so enables them to survive, and avoid the suffering and hardships that are their lot by nature. By forming a society in which everyone matters, and suffering is the greatest evil and pity the greatest good, those who suffer become the most important members, precisely because they are the weakest and most insignificant human beings.

For Nietzsche, belief in equality and the need for patience, understanding and compassion hold back the human race; it mediocritizes it, debases its value, and undermines the natural order. Only if the strong are allowed to lead, and we are brave enough to let the weak suffer and be slaves, can human beings advance as a species, true to themselves and the nature of existence. The new philosophers realize (Sections 1, 2, 5 and 6) that greatness consists in being noble, for oneself, bold, independent and complex, but with a singleness and strength of determination and will. The new philosophers are thus leaders, who, embodying the free spirit, introduce values from beyond good and evil, and discover and create new truths for human beings, which they lay down as laws for us, in a way that is consistent with the fact that their will to truth is a will to power.

Exploring the labyrinth of thought in *Beyond Good and Evil* reveals much that is interesting and also bewildering. It becomes clear why Nietzsche is regarded as such a complicated, important and controversial philosopher, whose thoughts cover a remarkable range of topics across science and the arts. His thinking has some surprisingly positive elements, which are often played down. For example, he wants us to recognize that we can never fully understand the world, and to realize that all our views about it suffer from a prejudice of perspective, which prevents them from being purely objective. He insists that all religions, philosophies and moral codes are at their most dangerous when they present themselves as the only truth, and he wants his readers to engage with the majestic complexity of existence, and not to hold back individual expression, which is often inhibited by bland social customs and expectations.

Of course, acknowledging these positive elements does not prevent critical assessment of his more unpleasant observations, most notably his theory (Section 9) that there are master and slave moralities, and his negative view of equality and pity. Here it appears that, for Nietzsche, human advancement is to be achieved, not through progress towards society's perfection, characterized by unlimited human love and democratic justice for all, but by returning to a more stark, brutal and (for him) more passionate and meaningful society of aristocratic hierarchy, like those of ancient Greece and Rome. He believes that aristocratic society, which demands slavery of one sort or another, has achieved every human advance. The 'slaves' invented the distinction between good and evil, and (as is consistent with his view of Christianity) sought to reverse the natural order, by claiming that those who instil fear (the strong, daring and powerful) are evil, when, according to master morality, 'good' people are those who instil (and want to instil) fear, while the 'bad' ones are the weak, suffering and despicable. Masterful people have no time for the distinction between good and evil; for them, there is only the difference between that which is good (themselves) and that which is bad (those below them). The designation 'evil' has helped to undermine the masterful, and allowed the slaves to pretend that suffering is good, when the truly good, the powerful and noble, rightly resent suffering and weakness, and have no time to pity or to be pitied. They find softer moral feelings as distasteful as the people who can only survive by exploiting them. Beyond good and evil, we must also disdain the thought that there is any moral worth in pity or altruistic behaviour.

Thus, Nietzsche does his best to undermine pride and confidence in the validity of our compassionate impulses. If suffering and inequality actually are necessary beyond good and evil, we may ask ourselves whether we really wish to accompany him beyond them. Even if he is right that these instincts are weak and unnatural, we may prefer them to endorsing suffering and injustice, even if it means not truly engaging with existence, or fooling ourselves. We might also ask whether true human strength and significance is to be found, not in succumbing to the inequalities, inherent in life, and using our power to be masters, but in resisting life's natural harshness, and fighting for what opposes it: love, patience and compassion. Certainly, it is legitimate to question whether or not Nietzsche is right that a true understanding of existence is to be found beyond good and evil. Perhaps, like the philosophers he censures, he is simply giving his own value judgements priority, and thus distorting the real nature and meaning of human life and the world.

Some Issues to Consider

- In *Beyond Good and Evil*, Nietzsche guides us through a history of human ideas and emotions, and their expression in philosophy, religion and society.

- He seems to want us to trust his view of the world, but also to be uncertain and wary of it; he encourages us to doubt, and then to doubt even the validity of our doubting, before we move 'beyond' with him.

- Nietzsche argues against philosophical and religious dogmatism, but seems to regard scepticism as equally undesirable: it demonstrates an animosity towards the spirit and the human will, analogous to that in Christianity and Buddhism.

- Nietzsche expects his 'new' philosophers to go beyond good and evil and the timid norms of received social and religious morality; as well as having a panoramic view of human existence, they must engage fully with life, and endure its tests and temptations.

- Nietzsche considers that the Christian saint's recognition that his will to power is satisfied in repressing the spirit is a shocking display of a religious neurosis, and criminal in the way that it resists and condemns desires that are natural to human beings.

- For Nietzsche, the spiritual life is the true, raw strength to live life as life, in a way that embodies the complex and frightening truths and absurdities of existence, from which we often try to escape.

- Nietzsche thinks that authentic human existence consists of being free to exist truly and magnificently as a collection of individuals, who are honest with themselves and the world.

- Nietzsche holds that there is nothing truly objective about any argument, no matter how much it is dressed up in dispassionate rationality or complex philosophical logic; that value judgements lie behind everything; and that they are biases, which lead thinkers, in their will to truth, to will one that confirms their particular prejudices.

- For Nietzsche, the new philosopher will reach the truth, and realize the true nature of existence, by understanding that human beings rely on untruths in order to comprehend the world.

- In Nietzsche's view, human beings (as in the philosophy of Descartes and Schopenhauer) seek to simplify everything, and, as a result, make existence less difficult, and so less magnificent, than it actually is.

- Nietzsche believes that the systems of thinking we have devised make it difficult for us to appreciate life fully, and live it properly: for example, life does not really throw up the question of whether the will is or is not free; in real life, it is only a matter of wills that are strong or weak.

- Is Nietzsche right to question whether such values as good and evil are really opposites and whether they really exist?

- Does it make any sense to talk of going beyond good and evil?

- Nietzsche criticized Plato's philosophy, but are there similarities between Nietzsche's moral theory, particularly in relation to master and slave morality, and some of Callicles' arguments in Plato's *Gorgias*?

- After being an early follower of Schopenhauer, Nietzsche eventually rejected the pessimism of his philosophy, but, paradoxically, questions the sincerity of Schopenhauer's pessimism in *Beyond Good and Evil*: is Nietzsche's own philosophy optimistic or pessimistic?

- Nietzsche criticizes the effect of value judgements on the way we look at the world; but to what extent is his criticism of, for example, pity the result of his own value judgements?

- Nietzsche is dismissive of democracy, and claims that it developed as a result of Christianity, which has turned values upside down, so that the weak and suffering have become the best and most worthy human beings, not the powerful and strong, who, by nature, are the most significant, and who should rule over the rest.

- To what extent would Nietzsche want us to resist our feelings of compassion; and does he think that they come naturally to us, or are the result of cultural indoctrination?

- Nietzsche associates all the human race's worthwhile achievements with the powerful and the strong, whose dominance in society involves the subordination and suffering of the weak.

- Nietzsche argues that the problem with his age is that the spirit is in crisis, as the triumph of Christianity and democracy has led to mediocrity and lack of individuality and vitality.

- Is Nietzsche right that only the weak need society, or does society try to enable all its members to thrive, by allowing individuals to pursue their own interests, such as raising families, creating wealth and gaining political power, which often benefit the whole community?

- Would Nietzsche argue that the only shared human interests are the will to truth and the will to power, which necessarily put individuals into competition with each other?

- While many of Nietzsche's views in *Beyond Good and Evil* seem unpleasant and highly disputable, the book contains positive elements and illuminating insights, which tend to be played down.

- Does Nietzsche, like the philosophers he censures, give priority to his own value judgements, and thus distort the real nature and meaning of human life and the world?

Suggestions for Further Reading

Friedrich Nietzsche, *Beyond Good and Evil*, trans. M. Faber, Oxford and New York: Oxford University Press, 1998.

Friedrich Nietzsche, *Human, All Too Human*, trans. M. Faber and S. Lehmann, London: Penguin, 1994.

Friedrich Nietzsche, *The Anti-Christ*, trans. H. L. Mencken, Tucson, AZ: Sharp Press, 1999.

Friedrich Nietzsche, *The Genealogy of Morals*, trans. H. Samuel and ed. T. N. R. Rogers, New York: Dover Publications, 2003.

Friedrich Nietzsche, *Thus Spake Zarathustra*, Ware: Wordsworth, 1997.

K. Ansell-Pearson, *How to Read Nietzsche*, London: Granta, 2005.

R. Descartes, *Discourse on Method and Meditations on First Philosophy*, trans. D. A. Cress, fourth edition, Indianapolis/Cambridge: Hackett Publishing Company, 1998.

A. Hoover, *Friedrich Nietzsche: His Life and Thought*, Westport, CT: Praeger, 1994.

I. Kant, *Critique of Pure Reason*, ed. V. Politis, London: Everyman, 1993.

L. Lampert, *Nietzsche's Task: An Interpretation of Beyond Good and Evil*, New Haven, CT: Yale University Press, 2001.

J. Locke, *Essay Concerning Human Understanding*, ed. R. S. Woolhouse, new edition, London: Penguin, 1998.

Plato, *Gorgias*, ed. R. Waterfield, Oxford and New York: Oxford University Press, 1998.

T. Roberts, *Contesting Spirit: Nietzsche, Affirmation, Religion*, Princeton, NJ: Princeton University Press, 1998.

A. Schopenhauer, *On the Basis of Morality*, trans. E. F. J. Payne, Providence, RI: Berghahn Books, 1995.

A. Schopenhauer, *The World as Will and Representation*, ed. E. F. J. Payne, Vol. 1, New York: Dover Publications, 1969.

G. B. Shaw, *Three Plays for Puritans*, London: Constable and Company, 1929.

B. Spinoza, *Ethics*, trans. E. M. Curley, London: Penguin, 1996.

Detailed Summary of Friedrich Nietzsche's *Beyond Good and Evil* (Sections 1–3, 5, 6 and 9: 257–70)

Preface (pp. 3–4)

If truth is a 'woman', philosophers, as '**dogmatists**', have courted her ineptly (p. 3). She has not been 'charmed', and 'dogmatism' is said to be 'defeated' (p. 3). Further, there is reason to hope that this type of philosophy was just the 'infantile high-mindedness of the beginner', and proof of the theory that 'all great things' first appear as 'monstrous and fear-inducing caricatures' of themselves, as in **Plato**'s doctrines of the '**pure spirit** and of **transcendental goodness**' (p. 3). They involved him in setting 'truth on its head', and denying '*perspectivity*' (p. 4). But it looks as if 'this error has been overcome', and the 'nightmare' will soon be over (pp. 3–4).

In Europe, the battle against Plato, or '**Christian-ecclesiastical pressure**' ('**Platonism for the "common people"**') has built up a 'splendid tension of the spirit', which will enable us to aim at very 'remote targets' (p. 4). For many 'Europeans', this 'tension' is distressing, and '**Jesuitism**' and the 'democratic **Enlightenment**' were attempts to 'loosen the bow' (p. 4). But those of us who are '*good Europeans*' and '*very* free spirits' have 'all the distress of the spirit', the 'tension' of the bow, the 'arrow' and the *'target . . .'* (p. 4).

Sils-Maria, Upper Engadine, June 1885

Section 1
On the Prejudices of Philosophers (pp. 5–24)

1 What sort of questions has the '**will to truth**', which leads us **philosophers** to undertake 'risky' adventures, and about which we speak deferentially, 'presented' to us (p. 5)? Already, it is 'a long story', but we seem to be just starting (p. 5). What impels us to 'get at the truth' (p. 5)? We spent a lot of time questioning this will's 'origin'; now we ask about its *'value'* (p. 5). Why do we not *'prefer* untruth', 'uncertainty' or 'ignorance' (p. 5)? Eventually, it seems as though 'the problem' has never been posed, and as if we are 'seeing it for the first time', and *'daring* it': no daring is 'greater' (p. 5).

2 How could 'something' originate in 'its opposite', for example, 'truth' in 'error', or **altruism** in **egoism** (p. 5)? It is 'impossible': things with the 'highest value' must have *'their own'* origin, which cannot be the 'perishable', 'deceptive, lowly world'; it must be the 'womb of existence', the '**"thing in itself"**' (pp. 5–6). But this is the **metaphysicians**' characteristic 'prejudice', which drives them to search for 'their "knowledge"', which they then describe as '"the truth"' (p. 6). Even though they have pledged that everything must be doubted, they do not doubt the *'opposition of values'* (p. 6). It does not occur to them that the existence of 'opposites' can be doubted, or that these 'value judgements' and 'oppositions' may be no more than 'temporary perspectives' (p. 6). We attach great 'value' to 'truth' and 'altruism', but should, perhaps, value 'appearance', the 'will to illusion' and 'egoism and desire' more highly; and,

perhaps, the 'value' of the former is due to their being '*related*', in 'an *insidious way*', to the latter (p. 6). We have to wait for a **new breed of 'philosophers'** (they are 'coming'), who will be 'philosophers of the dangerous Perhaps' (p. 6).

3 I consider most 'conscious thinking', including the 'philosophical', to be an '**instinctual activity**' (p. 7). A fresh understanding of 'heredity and the "innate"' is required here: his 'instincts' direct the bulk of a 'philosopher's conscious thinking' (p. 7). 'Value judgements', or, more precisely, the '**physiological' imperative** to preserve a 'particular kind of life', as in the views that 'certainty' has greater value than 'uncertainty', and 'truth' more than 'appearance', underlie 'all **logic**': but, unless man is the 'measure of all things', these may be mere '**foreground evaluations**', needed to preserve 'beings like us' (p. 7).

4 Our concern is not with a judgement's truth or falsity, but its tendency to preserve 'life' and 'the species'; we regard the 'most false' judgements, '**synthetic a priori**' ones, as the 'most indispensable' (p. 7). We believe we could not survive without 'logical fictions' and continually falsifying 'the world' by 'number' (p. 7). Accepting 'untruth as a condition of life' is to 'resist familiar values' in a dangerous way, and 'a philosophy' daring to do so puts itself '**beyond good and evil**' (p. 7).

5 What leads us to regard 'philosophers' with 'distrust and contempt' is not their being guileless and childish, but their lack of honesty (p. 8). They make out that they reach 'their opinions' through independently 'unravelling' a 'cold, pure' '**dialectic**', but, in reality, they are finding 'reasons' to justify a 'pre-existing tenet', and putting forward an 'abstract version' of 'their heart's desire' (p. 8). They are 'wily spokesmen' for their 'prejudices', which they call 'truths' (p. 8). We have the sight of '**Kant**'s hypocrisy', as he entices us down the

'dialectical backroads' to his '**categorical imperative**', and the 'hocus-pocus of mathematical form', in which **Spinoza** cloaks his philosophy, in order to make it proof against critics, thus highlighting his own 'timidity and assailability' (p. 8).

6 I have gradually come to realize what 'every great philosophy' is: its author's 'personal confession', originating from the 'moral (or immoral) aims' in it (p. 8). When he attempts to explain the most 'far-fetched metaphysical propositions', we need to ask what 'morality' the philosopher aims at (p. 9). The 'instinct for knowledge' is not philosophy's 'father'; rather, another 'instinct' has made 'knowledge' its 'tool' (p. 9). Indeed, every human instinct practises philosophy, as it wishes to portray itself as existence's 'ultimate aim' and the '*master*' of all the others: all our instincts are 'tyrannical' and seek to 'philosophize' (p. 9).

'Truly scientific people' may have an 'instinct for knowledge', which operates without engaging the 'other instincts' (p. 9). And it does not matter to which 'branch of science' such promising workers apply this instinct: they are not marked out by what they 'eventually' become (p. 9). But there is nothing 'impersonal' about the philosopher: his 'morality' determines '*who he is*' and the order in which the 'innermost drives of his nature' are organized (p. 9).

7 Philosophers can be 'malicious': **Epicurus**, for example, called Plato and his followers 'flatterers of **Dionysius**', suggesting that they were actors and lacked genuineness (p. 9). Epicurus was irked by the 'grandiosity' and 'theatricality' that Plato and 'his pupils' exhibited, while he hid himself away, and wrote hundreds of books (pp. 9–10). It took Greece a 'hundred years' to appreciate who he was (p. 10).

8 In every philosophical work, the philosopher's convictions make their entry.

9 There is 'deceit' in the **Stoics'** exhortation to '*live* "according to nature"' (p. 10). One who did so would be 'prodigal beyond measure', lacking 'purpose', 'conscience', 'compassion' or 'fairness' (p. 10). It would be impossible to live according to such 'Indifference'; living, which involves 'weighing', 'preferring' and 'wanting to be Different', is to wish to be 'other than' nature (p. 10). But, if living according to nature means only 'according to life', it is impossible to 'do *otherwise*' (p. 10).

Those who profess this doctrine actually want 'something' quite different: to 'dictate' their 'morality' and 'ideals' to 'nature', to remake it 'according to Stoics', so that it glorifies and universalizes 'Stoicism' (p. 10). They gaze uninterruptedly at nature, but 'see it *falsely*', 'stoically', and then cling to the 'lunatic hope' that, '*because*' they can 'tyrannize' themselves, they can do the same with nature (pp. 10–11). But what happened at the time of 'the Stoics' happens over and over again, as soon as philosophy starts to 'believe in itself': philosophy, the 'most spiritual form of the **will to power**', shapes the world in 'its own image' (p. 11).

10 In Europe today, we are forever discussing the issue of 'the real' and 'apparent world', but those who hear only a 'will to truth' lack sharp 'ears' (p. 11). There may be a few 'puritanical fanatics of conscience', who would prefer 'a certain Nothing' to 'an uncertain Something', but this is '**nihilism**', indicating a 'despairing, mortally weary soul' (p. 11). More energetic 'thinkers' align themselves '*against* appearance', arrogantly pronounce 'the word "perspectivist"', and seem willing to relinquish their 'surest possession', their 'bodies' (p. 11). Perhaps, at root, they wish to 'regain' that which was once 'possessed' even more certainly, and which produced a 'better' life than 'modern ideas': the '**immortal soul**' or 'the **old god**' (p. 11). Modern ideas are mistrusted; there is contempt for the '**eclectic**

conceptual bric-a-brac' of current **'positivism'** and the **'reality-philosophists'** (p. 11–12). We can say this of today's **'sceptical anti-realists'**: they see no reason to resist their impulse to get away from *'modern* reality'; but, with a bit *'more* strength', they would desire to 'go *beyond* – and not back' (p. 12).

11 Today, Kant's 'real influence on German philosophy' seems to be missed: he was proudest of his **'table of categories'**, which he regarded as the hardest thing done for metaphysics' 'benefit' (p. 12). But what he was taking pride in was discovery of a new human **'faculty'**, that of making 'synthetic a priori judgements'; and German philosophy's flowering stemmed from 'his disciples' vying to 'discover' something in which equal pride could be taken, or, at least, 'new faculties' (p. 12). But what does Kant's achievement amount to? He concluded (although he did not express it in 'four words') that synthetic *a priori* judgements were *'facilitated by a faculty'*; and the 're-joicing' was even greater (Germans had not yet become **'real-political'**) when he 'discovered a **moral faculty**' too (pp. 12–3).

So all the 'young theologians' (the distinction between 'find-ing' and 'inventing' had not been 'learned') of the **'Tubingen Stift'** searched for 'faculties' (p. 13). They identified one for the **'extra-sensual'**, which **Schelling** termed **'intellectual intu-ition'** (p. 13). But one must not flatter this 'movement' by tak-ing it 'seriously'; people woke up, and the 'dream vanished' (p. 13). What sort of explanation is it to say, as Kant did, that something is 'facilitated by a faculty': it just repeats 'the ques-tion' (p. 13). We ask, for example, how 'opium' makes us sleep, and are told that 'a faculty' facilitates it (p. 13). We must coun-ter Kant's question about the possibility of synthetic *a priori* judgements with one of our own: why is 'belief' in them *'neces-sary'* (p. 13)? It is because, although they could be *'false'*, we have to believe in their truth, in order to preserve 'creatures of our kind'; we are not entitled to them, but they are one of our 'foreground beliefs' (p. 13). And people were 'delighted' that 'German philosophy' had an 'antidote to the still overpowering **sensualism**' flowing into 'this century' from the 'previous one' (pp. 13–14).

12 Nothing has been so 'well refuted' as 'materialistic **atomism**', for which we are indebted to **Boscovich**, who disabused us of our belief in '**substance**', and **Copernicus**, who convinced us that the earth 'does *not* stand still': they both successfully opposed the 'appearance of things' (p. 14). However, the battle against the '**atomistic need**', which persists, must go on, starting with **Christianity**'s 'ominous atomism': that '*of the soul*', as something '**ineradicable, eternal, indivisible, a monad, an atom**' (p. 14). This does not mean we have to dispense with one of our 'oldest, most venerable hypotheses'; what we require are 'new and refined versions' of it, such as, perhaps, the 'mortal soul', the soul as the 'multiplicity of the subject' or as the 'social construct of drives and emotions' (p. 14). Thus, science can drive out the 'superstitions' that have multiplied around the 'idea of the soul' (p. 15).

13 What 'living' beings most want is to '*release*' their 'strength'; life is 'the will to power' (p. 15). '**Physiologists**' should reconsider their view that 'self-preservation' is the 'primary instinct' (p. 15). We must watch out for '*superfluous* **teleological** principles', such as this one, which is due to **Spinoza's** '**inconsistency**' (p. 15).

14 A few 'thinkers' seem to realize that 'physics' is a way of 'interpreting', not 'explaining', the world; but its reliance on 'belief in the senses' makes it seem something more: what is 'clear' and 'clarifies' is that which can be 'seen and touched' (p. 15). The '**Platonic**' **method**'s 'magic' is its '*resistance to* sensuality'; its practitioners looked for the 'higher triumph' of overcoming them, by spreading 'cold, grey **nets of concepts**' over what Plato termed the '**rabble of the senses**' (p. 15). Plato's interpretation of 'the world' differs from that of 'the physicists', including '**Darwinists**' and '**anti-teleologists**' (p. 16). Their 'principle', that human beings have nothing more 'to seek', if they have nothing else to 'see and grasp', is very different from his (p. 16).

15 To 'practise physiology' conscientiously, you must not regard the 'sense organs' as 'phenomena in the **philosophical idealist** sense'; they could not then be 'causes' (p. 16). Some argue that our sense organs create the 'external world', but this would make our bodies their creation, too: which, taking '*causa sui*' to be 'completely absurd', is a '*reductio ad absurdum*' (p. 16).

16 There are 'harmless self-scrutinizers', who believe in 'immediate certainties', such as '**I think**' or **Schopenhauer**'s '**I will**', as if 'perception could grasp' the 'thing in itself' (p. 16). Whatever 'common people' believe, the philosopher must recognize that the proposition, 'I think', involves a number of 'assertions' that cannot be proved: for example, that '*I*' am the 'thinking' one; that it is an 'activity and an effect' of a 'being', regarded as 'a cause'; that 'an "I" exists'; and so on (pp. 16–17). Again, when I say 'I think', I am '*comparing* my present state' to others: my referring back to 'another "knowledge"' indicates that there is no 'immediate "certainty"' (p. 17). What confronts philosophers here is a 'series of metaphysical questions' concerning the origin of the 'concept of thinking'; the reasons for belief in 'cause and effect'; and the 'right to talk about an "I"' (p. 17). Attempting to deal with these questions, by invoking some sort of 'epistemological *intuition*', as in claiming that 'I think' is 'true, real, and certain', will be challenged by today's philosophers (p. 17).

17 'Superstitious' logicians do not wish to admit that a 'thought comes' when 'it' wishes, not when 'I' do, so it falsifies 'the facts' to state that 'I' is the 'condition of the predicate "think"' (p. 17). The 'I' is a 'hypothesis', not an 'immediate certainty', and even to say 'there is thinking' involves 'an *interpretation*' (p. 17). The reasoning process runs along the lines that 'thinking is an activity'; for 'each activity there is someone who acts'; and so on (p. 17).

18 Being 'refutable' makes a theory 'charming': that of '**free will**' has been refuted many times, but endures due to 'this charm' (p. 18).

19 Philosophers, as in the case of Schopenhauer, talk of 'the will' as if the whole world knows about it; but he is taking up and 'exaggerating' a '*common prejudice*' (p. 18). Willing is '*complicated*', having 'unity only as a word' (p. 18). An act of willing involves a 'multiplicity of feelings', including a 'concomitant' one in 'the muscles' (p. 18). It also involves a 'commanding thought', which cannot be 'separated' from it (p. 18). It is 'an *emotion*', too: so-called '**freedom of the will**' is the 'emotion of superiority' to 'the one' having to obey (p. 19). Willing involves a concentration on the thing that must be had, and an 'inner certainty' of 'obedience': one who wills commands 'Something in himself that obeys', or which he believes will (p. 19).

We 'obey', as well as 'command', and experience 'coercion', 'oppression' and 'resistance' after 'the act of will'; but, through the '**synthetic concept "I"**', we overlook 'this division' (p. 19). We now believe that 'willing' is sufficient for 'action', and, because we expect obedience to 'follow' the command, we regard it as 'a *necessary effect*'; we consider 'will and action' to be 'one' (p. 19). 'Freedom of the will' refers to the 'complex pleasurable condition' of the 'person willing', who both

29

'commands' and, as 'under-soul', obeys: our bodies are social structures of 'many souls' (p. 19). And this is what happens in 'well-structured happy' communities, where the 'ruling class identifies' with the whole community's 'successes' (pp. 19–20). Willing is 'commanding and obeying', and the philosopher can understand it from 'within the sphere of ethics', which is the 'theory of hierarchical relationships', among which 'life' originates (p. 20).

20 'Philosophical concepts' do not just suddenly appear, but develop in relation to one other (p. 20). However apparently 'independent' of, and different from, each other, they follow each other 'in a certain order' (p. 20). 'Philosophizing' is '**atavism** of the highest order', in which 'concepts' are recognized and remembered 'anew': hence, the 'family resemblance' of 'Indian, Greek, and German' philosophy (p. 20). Where there is 'linguistic affinity', 'analogous' philosophical developments occur, while other interpretations of 'the world' are ruled out (pp. 20–1). Thus, '**Locke**'s superficiality' about the '**origin of ideas**' must be rejected (p. 21).

21 The idea of '*causa sui*' is contradictory, but 'excessive' human pride makes it hard to resist (p. 21). Our longing for 'free will', so that we can take full 'responsibility' for our actions is another form of it (p. 21). We should rid ourselves of this 'non-concept' and its opposite, the 'unfree will' (p. 21). Our error is the natural scientists' one of '*concretizing*' cause and effect: these are 'conventional fictions', whose 'purpose' is 'description or communication', not 'explanation' (p. 21). 'Causes', 'freedom', 'reason': they are our inventions, and, if we think that our 'world of signs' is what the world is 'in itself', we act '*mythologically*'; in 'real life', there is no 'unfree will', only '*strong* and *weak*' ones (p. 21). When someone detects 'coercion' or 'constraint' in a 'causal connection', it indicates

'his own inadequacy' (pp. 21–2). 'Constraint of the will' is always treated as a '*personal*' problem, whether by those with self-belief, who want 'credit' for everything, or by those whose 'self-contempt' impels them to repudiate any responsibility (p. 22). When such 'weak-willed' people write 'books', they often adopt '**socialistic compassion**'; and their '**fatalism**' looks 'prettier' when presented as a religion of suffering humanity (p. 22).

22 An 'old **philologist**' cannot help drawing attention to 'bad interpretative practice', as when 'physicists' talk of nature's 'lawfulness' (p. 22). This is not a matter of fact, but a 'naïve humanitarian concoction', which makes it possible to accommodate current 'democratic instincts' (p. 22). Everywhere, there is 'equality before the law', so it must be the same with nature; but natural 'phenomena' can be interpreted, equally as convincingly, as the 'ruthlessly tyrannical and unrelenting assertion of power claims'; as manifestations of the 'will to power' (p. 22). But such an interpretation would also claim that the world is 'necessary' and 'predictable', not because 'laws' operate in it, but because they are completely absent (p. 23). However, they are both just interpretations.

23 Up to now, 'psychology' has been halted by 'moral prejudices and fears', so no one has approached these matters, as I have, as a '**morphology and *evolutionary theory of the will to power**' (p. 23). A true '**physio-psychology**' must do battle with the researcher's 'unconscious resistances': the 'conscience' is offended by a 'theory' of the '"good" and "bad"' instincts' '**reciprocal conditionality**', and even more by the idea of the former deriving from the latter (p. 23). But 'hatred, envy, greed, power hunger' are 'fundamental' to life, and must be 'intensified', if life is going to be (p. 23). We are going to journey '*beyond* morality', and may, in the process, 'crush' what remains of it

(pp. 23–4). However, there have never been *'deeper'* insights, and the psychologist, who makes this sort of 'sacrifice', may insist that psychology be acknowledged as the 'queen of the sciences' and the route to 'basic issues' (p. 24).

Section 2
The Free Spirit (pp. 25–42)

24 We have clung to 'ignorance', to lead free, thoughtless and careless lives (p. 25). We could only base 'our science' on such ignorance while the basis of our 'will to knowledge' is 'no knowledge', 'uncertainty' and 'untruth' (p. 25). Even though we who know discover that our 'words' are distorted by deep-seated 'moral hypocrisy', occasionally we grasp what has occurred, and 'laugh' at how even the 'best science loves error', and keeps us prisoners in this 'neatly falsified world' (p. 25).

25 Philosophers must not defend themselves or be 'martyrs', as they will spoil the 'objectivity' of their consciences, and become 'stupid, brutish, and bullish', through fighting 'defamation' and 'accusations' (pp. 25–6). They do not have to be 'defenders of truth on earth', as if it needed 'defenders' (p. 26)! You know that it matters not whether *'you* are proved right': up to now, 'no philosopher' has been (p. 26). Instead, 'flee to hidden spaces' (p. 26)! One becomes 'venomous' and 'bad' in lengthy wars that cannot be fought openly (p. 26). In spite of their 'spiritual disguises', the 'long-term fugitives', and the 'enforced hermits', like Spinoza and **Brunos**, turn into 'elegant avengers and poisoners'; and then there is 'foolish moral indignation', which marks out a philosopher who has lost his 'philosophical humour' (p. 26). The philosopher's 'sacrifice for truth' brings out the 'propagandist and the actor' in him, and, while people have seen him as just an 'artistic curiosity', understandably, they now want to see him 'in his degeneracy' (pp. 26–7). Will this prove that the 'long tragedy' (assuming every philosophy, as it takes shape, is one) '*is over*' (p. 27)?

26 An 'exceptional person' seeks a place of refuge from the 'rule of "humanity"', but one factor impels him towards it: interacting with 'other people' may cause distress, but 'evading it' means not being equipped for 'knowledge' (p. 27). He will have to set aside his 'good taste', recognizing that the 'rule' is 'more interesting than the exception' (p. 27). Studying the '*average* man' is a 'serious' activity, and, though 'unpleasant' and disappointing, is essential for every philosopher (p. 27). But he may encounter 'so-called **cynics**', who will make his task easier: they recognize what is 'common, the "rule" about themselves', but have sufficient 'spirituality' to want to discuss it openly (p. 27). Cynicism is the 'form' in which 'common souls' come close to honesty: we find an 'exceptional mind' above a 'common heart' (pp. 27–8). The 'lover of knowledge' must listen attentively when someone talks 'badly', but 'without indignation', of humans, as if their only 'motives' are 'hunger, sexual desire, and vanity' (p. 28). In 'moral terms', 'indignant' people may rank above the 'self-satisfied **satyr**', but are 'more common' and less instructive (p. 28).

27 Living among those who live like 'frogs' makes it 'hard' to be 'understood', so we are indebted to those who attain 'subtlety' as interpreters (p. 28). However, 'good friends' are 'too comfortable', so, to begin with, we should allow them space for 'misunderstanding' (p. 28). This will give an opportunity 'for laughing', and (which we can also laugh about) we may be able to dispense with them 'entirely' (pp. 28–9).

28 It is very difficult to 'translate' the 'tempo' of one language's 'style' into another, and some well-meant 'translations' are virtual 'crudifications of the original', due to this failure (p. 29). This is a problem for Germans, who are 'incapable' of many of the diverting 'nuances' of 'free-spirited thought', as in **Aristophanes** and **Petronius** (p. 29). They tend to the 'solemn' and 'clumsy', **Goethe** not being excepted (p. 29). **Lessing**, with his 'actor's nature', is: he 'translated **Bayle**', enjoyed '**Diderot** and **Voltaire**', and adored '**freethinking**' and escaping from Germany (p. 29). But how could even Lessing's 'prose' attain **Machiavelli**'s 'tempo' in the '*Prince*', in which the 'most serious business' is put to a 'galloping tempo' of the 'most mischievous mood' (p. 29). Who would attempt to translate Petronius, whose work has the 'liberating mockery of a wind', into German; or Aristophanes, for whose sake one '*forgives* all of ancient Greece for existing' (pp. 29–30), provided one appreciates what needs 'forgiving' and 'transfiguring'. Nothing has led me to reflect on '*Plato's* opaqueness' more than the little story that he had a copy of Aristophanes under his 'death bed': even he could not have 'endured life' without it (p. 30).

29 Only a few strong people can be 'independent', and when this is 'attempted' by one not needing to be, he is 'probably' also recklessly 'bold' (p. 30). As no one sees where 'he is going astray', he is likely to perish; he is so remote from human 'understanding' that they neither 'feel it', nor 'feel for him' (p. 30).

30 Our 'loftiest insights' appear 'foolish' to those not equipped to hear them (p. 30). Whereas the '**exoteric** philosopher' not only 'sees' and 'makes judgements from the outside', but 'from down below', the '**esoteric**' one does so '*from above*' (p. 30–1). The 'soul' can attain 'heights' from which 'even tragedy' no longer has a 'tragic effect', so who can determine whether it should elicit 'pity in particular' (p. 31)? An ordinary man's '**virtues**' might be a philosopher's 'vices' (p. 31). Books

exist which have an 'inverse value for body and soul', in accordance with their use by 'lower' or 'higher' life forces: with the
former, they are 'dangerous' and 'disintegrative', but, with the
latter, 'calls' to 'valour' (p. 31). An 'odour of little people' clings
to common people's books, eating-places, even places of worship (p. 31).

31 When 'young', we indulge and abuse our 'taste for the
unconditional' (p. 31). Habitually angry and awe-struck youth
falsify 'people and things', to 'vent their feelings on them'
(p. 31). After the torture of 'unrelieved disappointments', our
young souls turn back 'suspiciously' on themselves, and we
'tear ourselves apart', as if 'our delusion' had been our choice
(pp. 31–2). Then we distrust 'our feelings'; feel 'our good conscience' is a 'danger', masking 'finer honesty'; and we 'take
sides *against* youth' (p. 32). Ten years later, we see that the
'whole process' was 'youth' (p. 32).

32 In the 'prehistoric age', 'consequences' decided an
'action's value' (p. 32). This was a *pre-moral* period', when no
one was aware of the 'imperative "know thyself!"' (p. 32). Sub-
sequently (and a 'refinement' in 'perceptions and standards'),
we have learned to determine an action's value by 'its origins'
(p. 32). This was the '*moral* period', indicating an effort at 'self-
knowledge' (p. 32). But the change was accompanied by a 'new
superstition': the narrow 'interpretation' of 'origin' as '*intention*' (p. 32). So, there was consensus that an action's value was
in the 'value of its intention' (p. 32).

Might we now be at the dawn of the '***extra-moral***' age (p. 33)?
We 'immoralists' suspect that an action's value is shown by
its non-intentional element: what is 'conscious' about it is
like its 'skin', hiding, rather than disclosing (p. 33). We think
that intentions need interpretation, and that 'intention-
morality' is a 'prejudice', which must be 'overcome' (p. 33).

This 'self-overcoming of morality' is a task reserved for to-day's most 'subtle and honest', if 'malicious', 'people of conscience' (p. 33).

33 We need to examine our 'feelings of devotion', of 'sacrifice for our neighbour', the 'morality of self-renunciation' and **'disinterested contemplation'** thoroughly (p. 33). Doing things for others', not one's own sake: such 'feelings' sound like '*seductions*' (p. 33). We may like them, but this is no 'argument *for* them', so let us be careful (p. 33).

34 Whatever our 'philosophical standpoint', the world's '*erroneousness*' strikes us; we may think there is something 'deceptive' in the 'nature of things' (p. 34). But, if we think that this 'falsity' is due to 'our thought process', that the world is 'falsely *inferred*', we have 'good reason' to doubt the 'thought process itself' (p. 34). And what assurance would there be that this would not continue? There is something 'touching' in the 'innocence' of those 'thinkers' who demand '*honest* answers from their consciousness', such as why it keeps the 'outside world' at 'a distance' (p. 34). But philosophers' 'faith' in 'immediate certainties' is 'stupid', and does us no 'honour' (p. 34). It may be that, in 'bourgeois life', 'distrust' is regarded as indicating 'bad character', but, today, the philosopher's '*duty*' is to be 'distrustful' (p. 34).

I now think differently about 'deceiving and being deceived' (p. 34). Regarding 'truth' as having greater value than 'appearance' is 'moral prejudice' (p. 34). There would be 'no life' without 'appearances'; and doing away with the 'apparent world' would mean no 'truth' either (p. 35). Why must we accept an 'essential difference' between truth and falsity (p. 35)? Why should there not be 'degrees of apparency' (p. 35)? The world that is '*relevant to us*' could be fictitious (p. 35). Any question about its 'author' could be 'part of the fiction' (p. 35). Are we philosophers permitted to be '**ironic**', not only about 'predicates and objects', but also 'subjects' (p. 35)?

35 'Truth', and the '*search*' for it, are not 'trivial' matters (p. 35). Going about the latter in 'too human' a manner will mean not finding anything (p. 35).

36 On the assumption that we are 'given' nothing 'real', except our 'world of desires and passions', and that the only 'reality' is that of 'our instincts', could this explain the 'material' world, not in the '**Berkeleian or Schopenhauerian sense**', but as one with the 'same level of reality' as 'emotion': a 'rudimentary form of the world of emotions', which holds the 'potential of the organic process' in a 'powerful unity', and in which 'all the organic functions' are 'synthetically linked' to each other (pp. 35–6)?

The 'conscience of our *method*' commands us to conduct such an 'experiment' (p. 36). We must not conclude that 'several' types of 'causality' exist, until we have checked that only one is not enough (p. 36). The question facing us is whether we accept the 'causality of the will', and we then need to determine whether this is the 'only causality' (p. 36). Wills, of course, can only affect other wills, not 'matter', so we are hypothesizing whether, wherever there are 'effects', one will is affecting another, and that all 'mechanical events' are actually the effects 'of the will' (p. 36). If our whole 'instinctual life', and 'all organic functions', could be explained as the 'development' of one 'basic form of the will', the 'will to power', and, through this discovery, we could solve the 'problem of procreation and alimentation', then we would be entitled to describe '*all* effective energy' as the '*will to power*': which would be the world 'described by its "**intelligible character**"' (p. 36).

37 Does not this mean that God, but not 'the devil', has been 'disproved' (p. 36)? 'On the contrary'! (p. 36)

38 Look what has happened with that 'gruesome' and 'superfluous farce', the **French Revolution**' (p. 37). Commentators have projected their own 'feelings' on to it for so long that *'the text has disappeared underneath the interpretation'* (p. 37). 'Posterity' could do this to the whole of 'history', to make 'the sight of it bearable' (p. 37). Has this not happened already, and, as we realize this, can we not stop it?

39 Nobody considers that a 'doctrine' is true just because it 'makes us happy or virtuous'; but, similarly, what makes us 'unhappy or evil' cannot be employed as a 'counter-argument' (p. 37). A 'harmful and dangerous' thing, which it might destroy us to understand, could nonetheless be true (p. 37). A person's strength of 'spirit' might be gauged by his capacity for tolerating undiluted and undisguised truth (p. 37). 'Wicked' people are better at discovering aspects of 'the truth'; and then ('moralists' say nothing about these) there are happy 'wicked people' (p. 37). It may be that 'harshness and cunning' favour cultivation of strength and independence of spirit more than the 'accommodating good nature' we value 'in scholars': taking it that we do not limit the 'concept of "philosopher"' to the writers of 'books' (pp. 37–8). **Stendhal** observed that a good philosopher should be dry, clear and illusion-free, having something of a banker's character.

40 Deep things love 'a mask' (p. 38). Some 'experiences' are so 'delicate' that they should be made 'unrecognizable' by being concealed as a 'coarse act' (p. 38). Some people know how to 'abuse their own memories', to 'take revenge on this one confidant' (p. 38). It is not the 'worst things' that make us most ashamed: it is not only 'wicked cunning' behind 'a mask'; there is 'so much kindness in cunning' (p. 38). One with 'deep' shame will hide his 'mortal danger' from his 'neighbours' and 'friends' (p. 38). Such a 'secretive one' asks that, in place of him, a mask inhabits his friends' 'hearts and minds' (p. 38). Every 'deep spirit' requires a 'mask'; and one is 'continually growing' there anyway, due to the '*shallow* interpretations' of everything he says and does (pp. 38–9).

41 We who are 'destined' to command must set tests for 'ourselves', and must not evade them, though we are the only 'judge' (p. 39). We must not rely on 'one person', 'a fatherland', 'pity', 'any science', or even 'our own detachment' (p. 39). We must not rely on 'our own virtues', nor sacrifice 'our wholeness' to 'some singularity about ourselves', such as practising 'liberality' until it turns into 'a vice' (p. 39). We must learn how to '*preserve ourselves*', the 'greatest test of independence' (p. 39).

42 A new 'category of philosophers' is coming, and although they wish, to a certain extent, to 'remain a riddle', I think they can be called '*experimenters*' (p. 39). But the name itself is an 'experiment' and 'temptation' (p. 39).

43 Are these 'approaching' philosophers 'new friends of "truth"' (p. 40)? Probably, and they are not 'dogmatists', as it would be against 'their pride' to impose 'their truth' on others (p. 40). We must free ourselves of the 'bad taste' of desiring agreement with 'many others' (p. 40). What of 'common goods' (p. 40)? It is a contradiction: what is 'common' lacks 'value' (p. 40). Ultimately, things will have to 'be as they are': 'the great' keep the 'great things', the 'abysses' are left to 'the profound', while 'everything extraordinary' remains with 'the extraordinary' (p. 40).

44 These 'philosophers of the future' will be '*very* free spirits', and more (p. 40). But, I must warn against a 'misunderstanding' of the 'free spirit' (p. 40). In 'Europe' and 'America', there are false so-called 'free spirits', 'loquacious' scribblers, who promote 'democratic taste' and 'modern ideas' (p. 40).

'Unfree' and 'superficial', they see the 'failure' of society's 'structures' as the source of '*all* human misery' (p. 41). With their slogans of 'Equal rights' and 'Compassion for all suffering', they are attempting to create a 'common green pasture of happiness for the herd' (p. 41).

In contrast, we know that the human 'plant' flourishes under 'the opposite conditions', and that 'pressure and discipline' make its 'spirit' more 'subtle and daring', intensifying it into 'unconditional power-will' (p. 41). Everything 'evil, frightful, tyrannical' heightens the human 'species', so we are the 'antipodes' of 'modern ideology' (p. 41). As 'free spirits', we are not 'communicative', having no desire to disclose what 'a spirit' can free itself '*from*', or be 'driven *to*' (p. 41). The 'dangerous phrase', 'beyond good and evil', protects us against misidentification, as modern 'freethinkers' (p. 41). We hate the 'temptations of dependence' that lurk in 'honours', 'money', 'position' or sensory 'enthusiasms', and are indebted to 'distress' and 'illnesses', which free us from a 'rule and its "prejudice"' (pp. 41–2). Our 'surplus of "free will"' prepares us for every adventure, while nobody can readily discern our 'ultimate intentions' (p. 42). We are 'friends of *solitude*' and 'free spirits'; and you 'approaching' *new* **philosophers** have 'something of it' (p. 42).

Section 3
The Religious Disposition (pp. 43–57)

45 For a 'born psychologist', the human soul's 'boundaries' and the inner life's 'dimensions' are the 'great hunt' (p. 43). But often he feels he is 'alone', and longs for, but has difficulty finding, 'helpers' (p. 43). There is no point sending scholars into these 'dangerous hunting grounds', for they lose their 'eye and sensitive nose' (p. 43). To grasp the history of such a 'problem' as '*cognizance and conscience*' in the soul of '*homines religiosi*', you would probably need **Pascal**'s 'monstrous' intellectual 'conscience' (p. 43). But you might wait for ever for suitable helpers: so, if there is something you want to know, you must do it '*yourself*' (p. 43). A 'curiosity' like mine is a 'pleasant' vice, or rather 'love of truth' brings its own 'reward' in 'heaven' and 'earth' (pp. 43–4).

46 The early Christians' 'faith', in a world containing different 'philosophical schools', and which had been taught tolerance by the Romans, was not like **Luther** or **Cromwell**'s 'naïve and quarrelsome' faith (p. 44). From the start, the 'Christian faith' has demanded the 'sacrifice' of 'freedom' and 'pride', and involved 'subjugation and self-derision', while assuming that 'submission of the spirit' is 'indescribably *painful*' (p. 44). These days, unlike the ancients, and 'deadened' to 'Christian language', we no longer appreciate the 'terrifying superlative' of the 'formula "**God on the Cross**"', which brought about a 're-evaluation' of 'ancient values' (p. 44). Thus, the 'Oriental slave' avenged himself on Rome's 'noble and frivolous tolerance'; it was their masters' 'smiling' indifference to the 'seriousness of faith' that inflamed the slaves, and turned them 'against their masters' (p. 44). 'Enlightenment' infuriates the slave, for, even in 'morality', he comprehends only the 'tyrannical', and fumes against the aristocrat's 'noble sensibility', which appears to '*deny* suffering': and this '**scepticism** about suffering' was a significant factor in causing the 'last great slave rebellion', which started with 'the French Revolution' (pp. 44–5).

47 'Solitude, fasting and sexual abstinence' always accompany appearance of the '**religious neurosis**': although another symptom is 'extravagant **voluptuousness**', succeeded by

'**penitence** and a denial of the world' (p. 45). But nothing has produced so much 'nonsense and superstition', and attracted so much interest, even from 'philosophers' (p. 45). Underlying 'recent philosophy', such as Schopenhauer's, are the issues of 'religious crisis' and 'awakening', of the possibility of denying 'the will', and 'sainthood' (p. 45). Unsurprisingly, Schopenhauer's most dedicated 'disciple', Richard **Wagner**, concluded his 'life's work', by bringing to 'the stage' that 'terrible and eternal archetype', '**Kundry**' (p. 45). The '**Salvation Army**' is the latest manifestation of the 'religious neurosis', available for psychiatric investigation (p. 45).

The 'phenomenon of the saint' has fascinated philosophers by its 'miraculousness', involving opposite 'conditions of the soul' with 'opposite moral value': a 'bad' person could become 'good' (pp. 45–6). But did not 'earlier psychology' make the mistake of *'believing'* in 'moral value oppositions', and 'reading' them into 'the case' (p. 46)?

48 'Catholicism' is more 'internalized' among the 'Latin races' than any type of **Protestant** 'Christianity' among northern Europeans (p. 46). In 'Catholic countries', not having faith is to rebel against the race's 'spirit', but, reflecting our 'barbarian' origins, for us 'northerners' it is returning to it (p. 46). The French, having a measure of 'Celtic blood' (in northern Europe, the **Celts** were most 'receptive' to 'Christian infection'), produce even 'sceptics' who are 'pious': there is something 'Catholic' and 'un-Germanic' in 'Auguste **Comte**'s sociology' and a 'Jesuitical smell to **Saint-Beuve**', while **Renan** is 'unintelligible' to our 'harsher' German soul (p. 46). His idea that religion is produced by a normal person, who is most right when most religious and assured of infinite life, is *'antipodal'* to my 'ears' (p. 47).

49 The 'ancient' Greeks' religious attitude was characterized by a 'wealth of gratitude'; only 'noble' people can 'face nature' thus (p. 47). The 'rabble' then gained control, and *'fear'* entered religion, preparing the way for 'Christianity' (p. 47).

50 A 'passion for God', like 'Luther's', which is that of an 'undeservedly' pardoned 'slave', is, like **Augustine**'s, 'boorish', 'naïve' and lacking in 'nobility' (p. 47). Curiously enough, it shows itself as 'the disguise' for a boy's or girl's 'puberty', or an old maid's 'hysteria' (p. 47).

51 The 'powerful' have shown respect for 'the saint' as a 'riddle' of 'self-discipline' and 'ultimate renunciation', sensing a 'superior force' behind his 'pitiable appearance' (p. 48). By honouring him, they also honoured 'something in themselves', yet they suspected an underlying reason for so great a 'denial': that a 'great danger' existed, of which 'the **ascetic**' was aware (p. 48). In his vicinity, the world's 'powerful' people became conscious of a new, 'unconquered' enemy: the 'will to power' (p. 48).

52 Nothing in 'Greek or Indian writing' can compare to the 'Jewish "Old Testament"' (p. 48). It puts us in touch with the 'tremendous remnants' of what humanity 'used to be' (p. 48). 'Tame' house-pets, such as today's 'civilized' Christians, will be unaffected by it: the Old Testament is a '**touchstone**' of 'greatness' or 'smallness' (p. 48). Their taste is more for that 'book of mercy', the 'New Testament', which reeks of 'devotees and small souls' (p. 48). This '**Rococo of sensibility**' has been joined with the Old Testament into the Bible, the 'book per se', which is 'literary' Europe's greatest 'sin against the spirit' (pp. 48–9).

53 Why does '**atheism**' now prevail (p. 49)? Because God does not 'hear'; does not communicate 'clearly' (p. 49). In Europe, while the 'religious instinct' shows strong growth, '**theism**' does not satisfy it (p. 49).

54 Since **Descartes**, philosophers have tried to destroy the 'old concept of the soul', the 'basic assumption' of Christian teaching (p. 49). '**Epistemological scepticism**' is '*anti-Christian*', though not 'anti-religious' (p. 49). Previously, people instinctively believed in the 'soul', holding that 'I' is a 'condition' and 'think' a 'conditioned' predicate (p. 49). Then, they wondered if the 'reverse' was the case, making 'I' a '**synthesis**', '*made*' through 'thinking itself' (p. 49). Kant wished to 'prove' that the 'subject' could not be 'proved' by 'means of the subject', and the 'object' could not be either (p. 49). He may have been aware of the subject or soul's '*apparent existence*', an idea present in the '**philosophy of Vedanta**' (p. 49).

55 Three aspects of 'religious cruelty' are particularly significant (p. 50). In ancient times, people sacrificed 'human beings' to their gods; at a later period in their moral development, their 'strongest instincts' or 'nature', as the 'celebratory joy' in the ascetic's face reveals (p. 50). What is then left is to 'sacrifice' the source of 'future bliss and justice': God; and all for the sake of 'nothingness' (p. 50). And this 'final', '**paradoxical** mystery' has been kept for the present 'generation' (p. 50).

56 One struggling with the need to 'think down' to the 'depths of pessimism', and save it from its 'half-Christian, half-German narrowness' of expression in Schopenhauer's 'philosophy', and who looks with '**super-Asiatic eye**' into the 'most world denying' of all 'ways of thinking' ('beyond good and evil', and not 'deluded' by 'morality', as are the '**Buddha** and Schopenhauer') will see the 'opposite ideal': that of a 'lively and world-affirming human being', who accepts, and wishes to have it 'over again', '*just as it was and is*', through 'eternity', that which 'has been and is', and who will call out '*da capo*' (p. 50). This will be '*circulus vitiosus deus*' (p. 51).

57 As the strength of a human being's 'intellectual sight and insight' develops, the 'space surrounding' him increases, and he comes across new 'images and riddles' (p. 51). Ultimately, all the most solemn concepts, such as 'God' and '**sin**', may seem no more 'important' than 'childhood' 'toys and pains' to an 'old man', who, an 'eternal child', will need 'different' ones (p. 51).

58 A 'true religious life', involving thorough 'self-examination' and 'prayer', to prepare for God's coming, demands 'leisure', so does not differ greatly from the aristocratic view that work 'debases soul and body' (p. 51). So, our present-day 'work ethic' acclimatizes us to 'lack of faith', and eliminates any conception of the 'possible use of religion' (p. 51). Apart from 'theologians', people today, including the 'majority of middle-class German Protestants', experience too many demands on their 'time' to have any to spare for 'religion' (pp. 51–2). They are not antagonistic to 'religious customs' if the state, for example, requires their participation in them, but are too remote from them to have 'their own Pro or Con' (p. 52). Nowadays, the 'German scholar' feels serenely benevolent towards religion, and finds it hard to take 'seriously' (p. 52). Even if historical study has led him to be grateful to religion, his 'practical indifference' towards it makes him avoid 'religious people or things', while his 'tolerance' of them is accompanied by a 'state of distress', which he seeks to escape (p. 52). The scholar's 'faith in his own superiority' is naïve, given that he is a 'presumptuous little dwarf and vulgarian', who produces 'modern ideas' (pp. 52–3).

59 Our 'instinct of preservation' leads us to be 'fleet, light and false' (p. 53). Those who need 'the surface' must, at one time, have grabbed beneath it (p. 53). Perhaps the 'born artists', whose sole pleasure seems to be falsification of 'life's image', 'belong to a hierarchy', and their 'degree' of sickness of life can be gauged by the extent of their desire to adulterate and dilute 'its image': the *'homines religiosi'* among the artists are those of the *'highest* class' (p. 53). For 'thousands of years', people's 'incurable pessimism' has compelled them to hold on to a 'religious interpretation of existence' (p. 53). So, 'piety, a "life with God"', seems to be the 'most exquisite' result of *'fear* of truth' (p. 53). It may be that piety is the most 'powerful device' for 'beautifying' human beings, as it can make them 'so completely into art' that no suffering is involved in looking 'at them' (p. 53).

60 Loving 'mankind' for God's *'sake'* has been human beings' 'most noble and far-fetched feeling': the idea that, without a 'sanctifying ulterior motive', loving people is just another 'brutish stupidity' (pp. 53–4). Whoever first had this thought should be venerated as one who has 'erred' in the most beautiful way (p. 54).

61 As 'free spirits', we see the 'philosopher' as one 'whose conscience' includes human beings' 'overall development', and who uses 'religions' as he does 'political and economic circumstances', to 'improve education and breeding' (p. 54). For the 'strong and independent', religion is one more way of surmounting 'obstacles' and learning 'to rule', tying 'rulers and subjects' together, and handing over to the first the second's 'consciences' and 'innermost secret': their desire to be free of having to obey (p. 54). If the higher 'spirituality' of some makes them prefer a 'contemplative life', religions can afford them rest, when faced by the *'cruder* type of authority', and 'purity', when confronted by the *'necessary* filth' of 'political activity'; thus, the **Brahmans** did, appointing kings, but remaining separate (p. 54).

Religion, by testing their 'self-control' and 'solitude', guides those of the 'governed', who wish to become leaders (p. 55). 'Asceticism and **puritanism**' are essential for educating and improving 'a race' desirous of overcoming its 'origin in the rabble' (p. 55). It also offers 'contentment' to those who exist to 'serve' and be 'useful', by justifying their 'everyday lives', and enabling them to 'bear the sight of themselves' (p. 55). It is the 'same effect' that 'Epicurean philosophy' has on 'higher class' sufferers: it refreshes, purifies and sanctifies suffering (p. 55). Perhaps, the most 'admirable' aspect of 'Christianity and **Buddhism**' is that they teach the 'lowliest people' that 'piety' gives them a position in an 'illusory higher order of things', thus reconciling them to the 'real order', in which their lives are 'harsh' (p. 55).

62 However, there is danger when 'religions hold sway', not as the philosopher intends, as a means for breeding and education, but *'absolutely'*, claiming to be 'an ultimate end' (p. 55). Even 'among humans', there is a 'surplus' of 'degenerating' and 'suffering' people, and the 'law of meaninglessness' has its most 'destructive' effects on 'higher individuals', whose 'needs' are hard to identify (pp. 55–6). These two 'greatest religions' attempt to retain what they can of the failures, regarding themselves as 'religions *for the suffering*', and treating those who 'suffer from life' as being 'in the right' (p. 56). While one admires their 'solicitude', particularly as it includes among those who suffer the 'highest species of humans', they have tended to preserve 'too much' of what should *'perish'* (p. 56). We are indebted to the 'spiritual people' of Christianity for what they have done for Europe, but, by the time they have comforted the suffering, and supported 'the dependent', what more could they do to ensure the *'degeneration of the European race'*: only 'twist' all that is 'masculine, triumphant, tyrannical', the love for 'earthly things' and for being the earth's master, into 'hatred of the earth and the earthly' (pp. 56–7)? Looking at Christianity's history in Europe, does it not seem that 'one will alone' has prevailed, and that it has been intent on making of humanity 'a *sublime deformity*' (p. 57). And would not someone with a 'divine hammer in his hand' look at the 'capriciously degenerate' being that is the 'European Christian', and protest angrily at the way in which his 'most beautiful stone' has been 'hacked' and 'bungled' (p. 57).

Due to Christianity, people who were neither 'strong nor far-sighted', and who were unable to allow the 'law of thousands of failures and defeats' to obtain, or to accept 'the gulf between human and human', were able to control 'Europe's destiny', and, with their insistence that people are 'equal in the eyes of God', breed a 'sickly' and 'mediocre' species, 'today's European . . .' (p. 57).

Section 5
Towards a Natural History of Morals (pp. 74–92)

186 Europe's current 'moral sensibility' is as 'subtle' and 'mature' as the 'science of morality' (an insufficiently 'modest' term) is 'raw' and 'crude'; this 'attractive antithesis' is sometimes found in the 'moralist' (p. 74). We should acknowledge what is needed in 'the long term', 'gather the material', and 'establish the concepts', in the 'area of values', to prepare for a '*taxonomy* of morals' (p. 74). Thus far, 'modesty' has been absent (p. 74). Once philosophers' concern was with 'morality as a science'; they sought to '*account*' for it, and think they have done so (p. 74). In their 'clumsy pride', they were far from the apparently 'modest', but essential task of 'description' (p. 74). 'Moral philosophers' knew the facts of morality 'only roughly', as the 'morality' of their 'class' or 'Church' (p. 74). Being

ill-informed about 'peoples' and 'past histories', they did not appreciate the 'real problems of morality', which become apparent only when '*many* moralities' are compared (pp. 74–5). What philosophers described as 'accounting for morality' was no more than a scholarly 'form of true *belief*' in 'prevailing morality', or a new way of '*expressing* it', and so was part of the situation within that 'morality': it was the 'opposite' of 'analysing' and 'doubting' their 'particular belief' (p. 75). Look at Schopenhauer's *The Fundamental Problems of Morality*, where he claims that 'all moralists' agree that harming no one, and helping everyone as much as possible, is the basis of morality and the principle they try to 'account for' (p. 75). We all know that he could not account for it, and also that it is a 'false' and 'sentimental' one in a world that has 'the will to power' as its 'essence' (p. 75). We should also ask Schopenhauer whether 'a pessimist', who 'denies God and the world', but who '*stops short* at the problem of morality', accepts a harm-no-one morality, and 'plays the flute', really is 'a pessimist' (p. 75).

187 As well as questions about its 'value', we can ask what an assertion, like 'a categorical imperative exists within us', says about the one asserting it (p. 75). Some 'moral codes' are intended to 'justify' their 'author' to others, some to 'nail him to the cross', some to enable the 'moralist' to 'exercise his power and creative whims' on other human beings (pp. 75–6). Through his code, Kant declares that what is 'honourable' about him is his ability to 'obey', and that it '*should* be' the same for everybody else (p. 76). Thus, 'moral codes' are just sign languages '*of emotions*' (p. 76).

188 Every 'moral code' opposed to '*laisser-aller*' is an instance of 'tyranny against "nature"' and 'reason'; but this objection would mean invoking another code, which prohibited 'tyranny and unreason' (p. 76). The 'essential' characteristic of every moral code is its being 'one long coercion', which is always used to achieve 'strength and freedom' (p. 76). 'Poets and orators' have had to submit to 'tyrannical laws', but the strange fact is that everything to do with 'freedom', 'daring' and 'perfect sureness', whether in 'ideas', 'governance', or 'oratory and rhetoric', has developed as a result of such 'laws': suggesting that they, not *'laisser-aller'*, is what is 'natural' (p. 76). It looks as if it is a 'protracted period of **unidirectional** *obedience'* that produces everything, such as 'virtue', 'art', 'reason' and 'spirituality', which make life 'worth living' (p. 77). 'Constraint of the spirit'; 'coercion'; the thinker having to work within a court's or church's 'guidelines'; having to find God in 'every chance incident': such 'violence', 'arbitrariness', 'harshness', although it 'suppressed' much 'energy and spirit', have made the 'European spirit' become 'strong' and 'ruthlessly curious', as thinkers understood what had to come out of their enquiries (p. 77). It seems that 'slavery' is 'indispensable' for disciplining and cultivating 'the spirit' (p. 77). Examination of any 'moral code' in this light makes us distrustful of *'laisser-aller'*, indicating narrower perspectives and being 'stupid' as preconditions of 'life and growth' (p. 77). A long period of obedience, without which 'self-respect' will be lost, is 'nature's moral imperative'; but it is not, as Kant insisted, 'categorical', and it is not 'addressed to individuals', but to 'peoples', to 'human beings *in general'* (pp. 77–8).

189 'Leisure' is burdensome for 'hard-working races' (p. 78). It was an English 'master stroke' to keep Sunday 'holy and humdrum', like a day of *'fasting'*, so that people would want to get back to work (p. 78). We need days of fasting, when 'powerful instincts and habits' can be 'fettered', and we can 'learn to feel hunger again' (p. 78). In history, we can see whole 'epochs' as times of 'coercion and fasting', when 'an instinct' is 'subjugated', but also *purified and intensified* (p. 78). This is a way to interpret a 'philosophical' sect, like 'the Stoics', which appeared in 'an **Hellenic culture**' that had become 'rank and surfeit' (p. 78). It also explains why, in 'Europe's most Christian period', and under the influence of its 'value judgements', the 'sexual drive was sublimated into love' (p. 78).

190 'Plato's morality' contains an element that is not 'part of' it: '**Socratism**' (p. 78). This includes the argument that no one desires to 'do himself harm', so it happens 'involuntarily' (p. 78). The 'bad man' would not do harm if he knew that 'bad was bad', and does so 'through error' (p. 78). By removing the error, we make him 'good' (p. 78). This line of argument focuses only on a bad action's 'nasty consequences': that it is *'stupid* to act badly', while what is 'good' is 'useful and pleasant' (pp. 78–9). Other forms of 'moral **utilitarianism**' have a 'similar origin' (p. 79). Plato did all he could to make Socrates' views 'subtle and noble', turning them into the 'infinite and impossible' (p. 79).

191 The 'theological' issue of '"faith" versus "knowledge"', of whether 'value judgements' confer greater 'authority' on 'instinct' or 'rationality', is the 'old moral problem' Socrates addressed, and which long predates 'Christianity' (p. 79). Socrates spent his life mocking the 'clumsy incompetence' of 'noble **Athenians**', all 'men of instinct', and at first sided with 'reason' (p. 79). But then, studying 'his conscience', he discovered a similar tendency in himself (p. 79). He concluded that we must 'follow our instincts', but persuade 'reason' to assist it with 'good arguments' (p. 79). Thus, the 'great ironist' made his 'conscience' accept 'self-deception': he realized the '**irrational aspect of moral judgements**' (p. 79).

Plato sought to prove that 'reason and instinct', left alone, aim at a 'single goal', the 'good' or 'God' (p. 80). Since then, 'theologians and philosophers' have followed the same path, and 'instinct', 'faith' or 'the herd' have triumphed in moral matters (p. 80). The 'exception' was the 'father of rationalism', Descartes: but 'reason' is just a 'tool' and Descartes was 'superficial' (p. 80).

192 Students of the history of science find it helps us to understand the 'common processes' in all 'knowledge and cognition' (p. 80). First, there are 'over-eager hypotheses' and absence of 'scepticism'; then 'our senses' develop greater caution (p. 80). We find it easier to 'reproduce' a familiar 'image' than to 'retain' what is 'divergent and new about an impression', while it is hard to hear what is new (p. 80). Our senses resist 'new things', while the 'emotions', such as 'fear, love, hatred', or mere 'laziness', tend to prevail (p. 80).

When reading, people barely distinguish five 'words' out of 'twenty', and hardly observe a tree 'completely' (pp. 80–1). We make up most of even our 'strangest experiences', and can rarely be compelled '*not* to observe' an event as 'its "inventor"' (p. 81). So, we are used to '*lying*', or, to put it less harshly, are 'artists much more than we realize' (p. 81). Conversing, I see my partner's face in terms of 'the thought' he expresses, or that I think I have elicited from him, in a way that exceeds my ability to see: he was probably making a 'different face, or none' (p. 81).

193 Our experiences in dreams are as much 'part' of our soul's 'economy' as what we actually experience, and make life 'richer or poorer' (p. 81). For example, if someone dreams that he is able 'to fly', this cannot but make his 'waking hours' happier, and what the poets call 'soaring' seem 'too earthly' (pp. 81–2).

194 Human 'diversity' is shown not only by differing tables 'of goods', and disputes about their 'comparative value', but by how people 'define *having* and *possessing*' them (p. 82). A 'modest man' will regard his sexual relationships with a woman as proving his possession of her; a more 'suspicious' one will want to be sure that she is 'giving up' all she has 'for his sake' (p. 82). An even more distrustful man wants her 'to know him thoroughly', including his 'devilishness', before accepting 'her love', so that she does not love a 'phantom' (p. 82). One man, who would like to 'possess a people', adopts the 'higher arts' of **Cagliostro** and **Catiline**; another is not satisfied that a mere 'mask of himself' should hold sway over 'his people', preferring 'to be known' and to know himself (p. 82). 'Helpful and benevolent people' often redraw the character of potential beneficiaries, to make them worthy of aid and 'deeply grateful', thus controlling 'the needy' like 'property' (pp. 82–3). Parents educate their children to resemble themselves, and subject them to their own 'concepts and judgements', as do 'teachers, classes, priests, and princes' (p. 83).

195 The 'Jews', whom Tacitus thought 'born into slavery', but who saw themselves as the 'chosen people', achieved a 'reversal of values' that made it possible for 'life on earth' to become newly and dangerously fascinating for up to 'two thousand years' (p. 83). Their 'prophets' brought 'rich', 'godless', 'evil', 'violent' and 'sensuous' together into a single 'entity', and first used the word 'world' as a 'curse' (p. 83). They treated 'poor' as a 'synonym' for 'saint': the *'slave revolt in morals'* originated with them (p. 83).

196 We can *'deduce'* that there are 'dark heavenly bodies' near to 'the sun' that we will never see (p. 83). This is 'a metaphor', and the 'moral psychologist' will read the 'celestial text' as one, a 'sign language' that keeps a lot 'in silence' (p. 83).

197 'Predatory' people and animals, such as Cesare **Borgia**, are misunderstood by 'moralists', who examine these 'healthy' creatures, to find their 'diseased state' (pp. 83–4). The 'tropical person' must be labelled as degenerate, while 'moderate', 'moral' and 'mediocre' people are favoured (p. 84).

198 Moral codes, 'addressed to individuals', and which aim at their 'so-called "happiness"', are 'behavioural guides', designed to 'counter' their 'passions', their 'will to power', if they want to be 'master' (p. 84). They are 'unreasonable', because they 'generalize' where they should not, and use 'unconditional language' (p. 84). By 'intellectual standards', all this is worth little, whatever 'form' it takes, whether a remedy against 'emotional folly', as 'advised by the Stoics', Spinoza's 'destruction of the emotions', or '**Aristotelianism**', a 'toning' down of them to a '**harmless mean**' (p. 84). It is neither 'science' nor 'wisdom', but a combination of 'shrewdness' and 'stupidity' (p. 84). It might be a morality of 'enjoyment of emotions', 'diluted and spiritualized' through 'art', 'love of God', or 'mankind for God's sake' (pp. 84–5). It could be, as Goethe suggested, 'wanton devotion to the emotions', a 'bold dropping of the reins' (p. 85).

199 There have always been 'human herds', and proportionately more 'followers' than 'commanders' (p. 85). As 'obedience' has been 'practised' so long among humans, it is a fair assumption that 'everyone' has an inborn 'need to obey' (p. 85). 'Human development' has been held back, even reversed, because the 'herd instinct of obedience' is 'inherited' at the expense of 'skill in commanding' (p. 85). There is a scarcity of 'commanders', or they feel bound to pretend not to issue 'commands' (p. 85). This is the commanders' 'moral hypocrisy', which is common in 'Europe today' (p. 85). Commanders have to make out that they are carrying out 'orders' from someone else, such as 'the constitution' or 'God', or profess that they are instruments 'for the common good' (p. 85). The 'herd man' has become self-important, parading his qualities of docility and usefulness to 'the herd', as if they were 'true human virtues' (p. 86). These days, people try to 'replace commanders' with a group of the 'cleverest herd people', which is the 'origin of all representative constitutions' (p. 86). The 'appearance of an absolute commander', like **Napoleon**, has a 'powerful' effect on the 'European herd animals' (p. 86). Its history is that of the 'higher happiness' the 'entire century' achieved in its 'most valuable people and moments' (p. 86).

200 One living in 'an age of disintegration', which 'mixes' races together, will bear the 'heritage of his multifarious origins', in the form of 'contradictory' and warring 'standards and instincts' (p. 86). Essentially 'weak', he will want 'the war' he *embodies* to end (p. 86). Agreeing with 'a mentality that tranquillizes', such as Christianity, he considers 'happiness' to be 'rest', the **'Sabbath of Sabbaths'** (p. 86). But, the 'warlike oppositions' inside him may stimulate him to live *'the more'*, and, if he has the 'expertise and cunning' to fight himself, he may become one of those 'unfathomable men', destined for 'victory' and 'seduction', such as **Alcibiades**, **Caesar**, **Frederick II** or **Leonardo da Vinci** (pp. 86–7). Both 'types' belong together, and 'arise from the same causes' (p. 87).

201 While the **'utility'** dominating 'moral judgements' remains that 'of the herd', and we limit ourselves to preserving 'the community', searching for 'immorality' in what endangers 'communal stability', there can be no 'morality of neighbourly love' (p. 87). The tiny acts of 'consideration', 'sympathy' and 'fairness', which will, in time, be described as 'virtues', are present, but are, as yet, *'extra-moral'* (p. 87). In Rome's 'heyday', an 'act of pity' was not 'good' or 'evil', but was disdained in comparison to an act that could benefit the whole commonwealth (p. 87). In the end, 'neighbourly love' takes second place to *'fear of one's neighbour'*: once there is security against 'external' threats, this is the issue that drives 'value judgements' (p. 87). Such 'dangerous instincts' as 'adventurousness', 'rapacity' and 'lust for power' were fostered as useful against 'common enemies', but now only their danger is appreciated, and they are 'stigmatized and slandered' (p. 87). The present moral outlook, born of the 'herd instinct', focuses on the harmfulness of anything to 'the community' and 'equality', so, again, 'fear is the mother of morality' (p. 88). Everything, even 'great powers of reason', which raises the 'individual above the herd', is seen as *'evil'* and condemned (p. 88). In extremely 'peaceable' conditions, any sternness or harshness is regarded as 'offensive' (p. 88). A point of such 'pampered indulgence' may be reached that society sides with 'the *criminal*', and considers punishing him to be 'unfair' (p. 88). We have the 'imperative' of 'herdlike timidity' (p. 88). We long to have nothing to fear; in today's Europe, the 'will and the way' towards it is called 'progress' (p. 88).

202 People do not want to hear *'our* truths'; and we will be thought *'criminal'* for using terms like 'herd' of those with 'modern ideas' (p. 89). We can do no other. Today's 'Europeans' know what 'Socrates thought he did not': what is 'good and evil' (p. 89). But it is the 'herd animal that thinks it knows', and calls itself 'good', so European morality today is *'herd animal morality'* (p. 89). It robustly 'defends itself' against other 'possibilities' (p. 89). With religion's support, we have 'Christianity's heir', the *'democratic* movement': the 'tempo' of which, judging by the 'increasingly frantic howl', is too 'slow' for its 'overeager' advocates (p. 89). They are against any 'form of society', apart from *'autonomous* herds', and seem

to be 'in conflict' with 'peaceably industrious democrats' (pp. 89–90). They are hostile to exceptional rights and privileges (indeed, to all, as no one needs 'rights', when all are 'equal'), and 'united' in 'their religion of pity' and 'mortal hatred of any suffering' (p. 90). They are committed to a *'communal* pity', as if it is 'Morality itself', and seem to want to subject Europe to a 'new Buddhism' (p. 90). What they hold to is 'belief in community as a *redeemer*', in 'the herd' and in 'themselves' (p. 90).

203 What 'hopes' do we have, who see the 'democratic movement' as a 'decadent form of political organization', which 'mediocritizes' human beings (p. 90)? We trust in the *'new philosophers'*, who will have sufficient strength and originality to oppose current 'value judgements'; to give a new direction to 'a thousand-year-old will'; and to lay the foundations for daring 'experiments in discipline and breeding', which will end the 'reign of nonsense and coincidence' we call 'history', of which the 'nonsense' about the **'greatest number'** is only the latest manifestation (pp. 90–1). For this, we need new 'philosophers and commanders', 'free spirits' who will 'feel *compelled*' to achieve a 'revaluation of values', and who will transform the 'conscience' into 'steel' and the 'heart into bronze', so as to carry the 'weight of such responsibility' (p. 91). The 'terrible danger', worrying and oppressing us, is that they might 'not arrive', or 'go astray' (p. 91). Nothing is more painful than to see an 'extraordinary man' going astray (p. 91). One who sees that '"man" himself is *degenerating*', and who foresees the outcome of the 'stupid innocence and blissful confidence of "modern ideas"' and 'Christian-European morality', endures an unparalleled 'anxiety' (p. 91). He sees what *'mankind could be bred to be'*, and how his 'greatest possibilities' stay 'untapped' (p. 91). Anyone aware of man's *'overall* *degeneration*', his 'diminution' into a 'perfect herd animal' (what the 'socialist fools' call a 'free society'), and who has thought through all the implications, must know 'no disgust but other people', and, perhaps, see 'a new *project*' (p. 92).

Section 6
We Scholars (pp. 93–108)

204 I want to 'argue against' a 'harmful **hierarchical shift**' between 'science and philosophy' (p. 93). I hold that someone's 'right to speak' about such a matter comes from '*experience*', which is invariably 'bad' (p. 93). **Science's 'Declaration of Independence' from 'philosophy'** is one of the 'more subtle influences of the democratic disposition' (p. 93). Here, too, is the 'urging' of the 'rabble instinct', and 'science', having freed itself from '**theology**', now wants to be 'master', and legislate for philosophy (p. 93). I have heard many 'naïve' and dismissive remarks about philosophy, from the 'colour-blindness of a utilitarian', who sees it only as a succession of '*refuted* systems', which serves no useful purpose, to 'disdain' for 'particular philosophers' and 'philosophy' generally (pp. 93–4). But, at the root of many young scholars' condescending attitude towards philosophy is the 'bad influence' of philosophers, who show contempt for their fellow philosophers' work (p. 94). Schopenhauer's treatment of **Hegel** tore a 'generation' of 'young Germans' away from their 'relation to German culture', which offered a '**supreme divinatory refinement of the *historical sense*'** (p. 94). Again, current philosophy's impoverished state has encouraged the 'rabble instinct': we lack philosophers of the calibre of Plato and **Heraclites** (p. 94). Nothing is more likely to produce a negative attitude towards philosophy, and '*disbelief*' in its 'masterfulness', in young science 'scholars and specialists', than the 'hodgepodge' of '"**reality philosophers**" or "positivists"' (p. 94). Science exudes 'good conscience', while philosophy has 'sunk to its dregs' (p. 95). Philosophy is 'at its last gasp': how can it *'be the master'* (p. 95)?

205 Today, a philosopher faces many 'dangers' (p. 95). The prodigious 'size' of the 'towers of knowledge' may exhaust him, while he is still learning, or lead him to 'specialize', so that he is never able to make a 'grand survey' of the whole subject (p. 95). If he reaches the 'top too late', his 'powers' will be too depleted for him to make a worthwhile 'overall value judgement' (p. 95). He may fear becoming a **'dilettante'**, or that loss of 'self-respect' will prevent his being a leader in the quest for 'knowledge' (p. 95). At the same time, he knows he must make 'a judgement', a 'Yes or No', not 'about the sciences', but 'about life' and its 'value': and he comes to realize that only 'wide-ranging' experiences, perhaps 'disruptive, destructive' ones, will equip him to do so (p. 95). A popular misconception is that philosophers, whether 'ideal' scholars, or religious enthusiasts, are men who live 'prudently and apart', and who have escaped the 'wicked game' of life (p. 96). In fact, the 'true philosopher' lives *'imprudently'* and 'continually' risks *'himself'* (p. 96).

206 A 'genius' is one who *'begets* or *gives birth'*, and, compared to such a one, the average 'scholar' is a bit of an 'old maid'; grudgingly, we confer 'respectability' on both (p. 96). What is a 'man of learning' (p. 96)? He is 'industrious', 'moderate' and conformist, desiring a degree of 'independence', a place to 'work in peace', and a 'good name'; this is the 'seal' upon his 'usefulness' that must 'overcome' the 'inner *mistrustfulness'* of all 'herd animals' (p. 96). But he is neither 'masterful' nor 'self-sufficient', and is prone to 'petty envy'

(p. 96). At his 'worst' and 'most dangerous', his instinctive 'mediocrity' ('Jesuitical', in that it knows how to 'present itself as a religion of pity') labours to 'destroy' and 'break' the 'extraordinary man' (p. 97).

207 We are rightly disgusted with 'subjectivity' and its 'damned **ipseity**', but, in our desire for objectivity, we must not, as the 'pessimists' do, over-praise 'intellectual selflessness and depersonalization', as if they were ends 'in themselves' (p. 97). True, the 'objective person', in whom the 'scientific instinct blossoms', is one of our 'most precious tools', but he needs direction by one 'more powerful' (p. 97). The 'objective man' is a *'mirror'*, whose only 'desire' is to reflect what 'knowledge' offers him (p. 97). He pays little attention to 'his own needs' or 'suffering', because his mind is always preoccupied with general cases (pp. 97–8). Welcoming 'all' experiences, he is dangerously unconcerned about 'Yes and No' (p. 98). If expected to show 'love or hatred', as understood by 'God, women and animals', he will do his best, but it is no surprise if the first is 'forced' and the second 'artificial' (p. 98). He is 'genuine' only if 'objective', and he does not know how to 'deny', 'command' or 'destroy' (p. 98). He is no 'model human being', for, having placed himself 'at such a distance', he has no basis for taking sides 'between good and evil' (p. 98). We 'honour' him too much, if we see him as a *'philosopher'*, a **'dictatorial breeder and tyrant of culture'**, for he is a 'slave-like entity' (p. 98). Though 'precious', he is not 'a goal', or one 'in whom the *rest* of existence is justified' (p. 98). He is neither a 'conclusion' nor even a 'beginning', for neither 'powerful' nor 'autonomous' he has no wish to be 'master'; like an empty 'vessel', he awaits a 'content', in order to '"take shape" accordingly' (pp. 98–9).

208 When a philosopher claims to be 'no sceptic', it pleases no one, but frightens 'timid listeners', who fear some 'intellectual dynamite', like a 'newly discovered **Russian nihilism**' (p. 99). There is 'no better sedative' than the 'lulling opium of scepticism', and the sceptics, friends of 'peace', point out that there are already 'enough bad noises' (p. 99). 'Yes! And No!' offend the sceptics' 'morality': like **Montaigne**, they prefer to wonder what they know, or, like **Socrates**, to say they 'know nothing' (p. 99). They think it 'better taste' not to advance any 'hypotheses', and are beguiled by uncertainty's 'charms' (pp. 99–100).

Sceptics need comforting, for 'scepticism' is the 'most spiritual expression' of what we call 'bad nerves' (p. 100). This manifests itself when long separated 'races or classes' suddenly 'intermix' (p. 100). In these situations, 'everything is restless, agitated, doubtful, experimental', but what tends to degenerate most is 'the *will*'; even when dreaming, people 'doubt "the freedom of the will"' (p. 100). The 'ridiculously sudden experiment' in radically mixing 'classes' and 'races', which present-day Europe is witnessing, is making it 'thoroughly sceptical' (p. 100). Everywhere, one stumbles across 'Paralysis of the will', although invariably decked out as 'objectivity' or 'scientific method' (p. 100).

This 'disease of the will' does not affect Europe evenly; it is at its most severe where 'culture' has been 'domesticated longest', but is less intense where the 'barbarian' still 'holds sway' (p. 100). It is 'sickest' in France, which displays the 'glamour of scepticism', 'stronger' in Germany, and, due to '**phlegm**' and 'hard heads' respectively, 'noticeably' more so in England and Spain (pp. 100–1). It is 'strongest' in Russia, where the will 'waits ominously to be released' (p. 101). So, it may not be only 'wars in India' and Asian 'entanglements' that are needed to 'relieve Europe of its greatest danger': it may not be to 'my liking', but the rise in the Russian 'threat' may become 'so great' that Europe will have to respond by employing a 'new ruling caste', in order to give it a 'long-lived will of its own' (p. 101). And this will involve ending its '**small-state system**' and the '**multiple wills**' of its '**dynasties and democracies**' (p. 101). By the 'next century', 'petty politics' will be exchanged for 'politics on a grand scale'; we will be fighting for 'mastery over the earth' (p. 101).

209 To what extent will Europe's coming 'warlike age' foster a 'different, stronger sort of scepticism' (p. 101)? That 'military and sceptical genius', King **Frederick William I** of Prussia, 'father of **Frederick the Great**', recognized Germany's 'deficiency': '*Men were lacking*' (pp. 101–2). Further, seeing him fall prey to 'atheism' and 'bloodsucking' scepticism, he feared his own son might not be 'enough of a man', and would lack a 'heart' that was tough enough 'for evil or for good' (p. 102). In fact, a new 'daring, manly scepticism', suited to 'war and conquest', and perhaps nourished by his 'father's hatred', was developing in Frederick (p. 102). This was scepticism in its '*German* form', which gives 'dangerous freedom' to the 'spirit', but keeps the heart 'sternly in line' (p. 102). By establishing a '*new* concept of the German spirit', with its fearlessness, tenacity and 'pronounced tendency to manly scepticism', this '**Frederickianism**' has brought Europe under the 'dominion of the German spirit' (p. 102). It is understandable that 'warm-blooded', 'superficial' people '**cross themselves**' when they encounter it, but it is not long since **Madame de Staël** suggested that Europe should be interested in the Germans as 'gentle, good-hearted, weak-willed and poetic fools', while Napoleon was astonished that Goethe was 'a *man*'; he had only expected to meet 'a German' (pp. 102–3).

210 When describing the 'philosophers of the future', we may wonder whether they will need to be 'sceptics' in the sense 'above' (p. 103). They would be entitled to call themselves 'critics'; and they will 'surely' be experimenters (p. 103). And will they, in their eager pursuit of 'knowledge', go further with their 'experiments' than this 'soft', 'democratic century' can allow (p. 103)?

Undoubtedly, these 'coming men' will be the 'least able' to relinquish the 'qualities' of 'certainty of standards', use of a 'unified method, shrewd courage, independence' and 'self-reliance', which distinguish the 'critic' from the 'sceptic' (p. 103). Assuredly, they will be *'harsher'* (and not just to 'themselves') than 'humane people' may like, and will not engage with 'truth' simply because they like it, or it exalts them; they will experience genuine 'disgust' for such 'enthusiasm, idealism' and 'femininity' (pp. 103–4). Their 'intention' will not be to reconcile 'Christian sentiment' with 'ancient taste' or 'modern parliamentarianism' (p. 104). They will be rigorous, but will not wish to be 'called critics', as they will think it insulting for philosophy to be regarded as a mere **critical science** (p. 104). Even though this 'evaluation of philosophy' may have pleased even the 'great' Kant (look at the **titles of his major works**'), these 'new philosophers' will regard 'critics' as the philosopher's 'tools', and so will not be ones themselves (p. 104).

211 We must shake off the view that '**philosophical workers**' are 'true' philosophers (p. 104). The latter's 'education' may necessitate their going through 'the stages' at which the former *'must* remain', and the true philosopher may need to have been many things, including 'critic', 'sceptic', 'puzzle-solver and moralist and seer'; but these are mere 'preconditions for his task', which is to *'create values'* (pp. 104–5). The philosophical workers, in the 'noble mould of Kant and

Hegel', have the job of describing, 'clearly' and 'intelligibly', the logical, political and **aesthetic** 'value judgements' of 'the entire past'; but '*true philosophers are commanders and lawgivers*' (p. 105). Using the philosophical workers' 'preparatory' labours, they 'reach towards the future', to lay down 'the way it *should* be!', and 'their will to truth is – *will to power*' (p. 105). Such philosophers '*have* to exist' (p. 105).

212 Being '*necessarily* a man of tomorrow and the day after', the philosopher is bound to be at odds with 'Today' (p. 105). Philosophers' 'difficult', 'unrefusable' and great task has been, by exposing the 'hypocrisy, smugness', '**casual acquiescence**', and the 'falsehood' of '**contemporary morality**', to be 'the **bad conscience of their age**', thus marking out a 'new, untrodden path to **human aggrandizement**' (pp. 105–6). Opposing 'modern ideas', which seek to limit everyone to a 'speciality', the philosopher must discover 'human greatness' in 'man's breadth and variety', in 'his **wholeness in diversity**' (p. 106). Today, 'weakness of will' is 'fashionable', but it is its 'strength', and the 'capacity for lengthy decisions' that are 'integral' to the philosopher's idea of human 'greatness' (p. 106). This is fitting, as, in the 'sixteenth century', the 'opposite doctrine', that of 'submissive, selfless humanity', created 'tidal waves of selfishness' (p. 106). In Socrates' day, for pleasure's sake, the 'Athenians let themselves go', while still mouthing the 'same splendid words' their 'lives' had long since 'failed to justify' (p. 106). Today's Europe honours only the 'herd animal', and 'equal rights' too 'easily' become 'equality of wrong', as they battle against all that is 'rare' and 'privileged': the higher 'soul', 'higher duty' and 'higher responsibility', and the 'creative abundance of power and elegance' (p. 106). So, today, being 'different', and living 'independently', are central to the 'concept of "greatness"' (p. 106). The philosopher proclaims

that the 'greatest person' is the one capable of being the most 'lonely', 'hidden' and 'deviant', who is 'beyond good and evil', and 'rich in will': *'greatness'* is being able to be **'multifarious and whole'** (pp. 106–7).

213 Learning what a philosopher is must be acquired 'from experience'; it 'cannot be taught' (p. 107). 'Popular opinions' about philosophy and philosophers are wrong, but, regrettably, everybody today speaks of things they *'cannot* have experienced' (p. 107). Few 'thinkers and scholars' have experienced the **'truly philosophical coexistence'** of **'unrestrained spirituality'** and **'unerring dialectical rigour'**, and would consider it 'unbelievable' (p. 107). They regard 'thinking itself' as 'almost an affliction', rather than being 'light' and 'divine' (p. 107). Perhaps, 'artists' have a better insight, and know that, when they do things 'by necessity', feelings of 'freedom' and creativity come into their own: 'necessity' and 'freedom of will' become 'one and the same' (p. 107). There is a 'hierarchy of inner states', corresponding to the 'hierarchy of problems', and the 'greatest' of the latter repel those not **preordained** to solve them' by their spirituality's 'greatness and power' (p. 107). It is pointless for 'ordinary minds', or even 'honest craftsmen and **empiricists'**, driven by **'plebeian ambition'**, to tackle these problems: the **'primordial law of things'** will prevent the 'intruders' from doing so (pp. 107–8). We must be 'born' and *'bred'* to every 'higher world' (p. 108). Our 'right to philosophy' comes from 'our origins': successive 'generations' must do the groundwork for the 'philosopher's development' (p. 108). His 'virtues' must be cultivated, and his 'readiness for great responsibilities' prepared (p. 108). He needs to feel separated from the 'masses' and their 'duties and virtues'; must enjoy and practise 'great justice'; and have the 'art of command' and 'expanse' of will (p. 108).

Section 9 (Paragraphs 257–70)
What is Noble? (pp. 151–67)

257 Aristocratic societies, with a hierarchy, which 'value' people differently and operate some form of 'slavery', were the ones that achieved every past 'elevation' of human beings, and they always will (p. 151). The 'ever greater distances within the soul itself', and 'spacious inner states', are not attainable without a *'grand feeling of distance'* **between classes**, with the 'ruling' class looking down at its 'underlings and tools' (p. 151). The 'truth' about the 'historical origins' of these 'higher' cultures is 'harsh': people with a 'natural' and 'predatory' nature, who were 'barbarians', attacked 'weaker, more well-behaved, peaceable' races, or cultures whose dissolution was marked by displays of 'wit and depravity' (p. 151). And to start with, the **'barbarian' caste**'s dominance was due to its 'spiritual', rather than 'physical strength': its members were *'more complete'* humans, and, therefore, 'beasts' (p. 151).

258 'Corruption', expressing 'impending anarchy' among the 'instincts' and the 'collapse' of life's 'emotional foundations', varies, reflecting the 'form of life', in which it shows itself (p. 152). It was 'corruption' when 'pre-Revolutionary' France's 'aristocracy' abandoned its 'privileges', and sacrificed itself to excessive 'moral feeling' (p. 152). This was the culmination of a process by which the aristocracy relinquished its 'tyrannical authority', and reduced itself to '**a** *function* **of the monarchy'** (p. 152). In contrast, a 'healthy aristocracy' regards itself as the *'essence'* of its society, and has no qualms about oppressing and diminishing 'incomplete people', as 'slaves' or 'tools', for its own 'sake' (p. 152). Its view is that society only exists as a means of enabling a 'select kind of creature' to rise to its 'higher task' and 'higher *existence'* (p. 152).

259 Refraining from 'injuring, abusing, or exploiting' others can lead to 'good manners between individuals', but should only be pursued if their 'strengths and standards' are 'similar', and they belong to a 'single social body' (p. 152). Turning this 'principle' into society's *'basic'* one would be a 'will to *deny* life', leading to 'dissolution and decline' (p. 152). Life's *'essence'* is to exploit and oppress the 'foreign and weaker' (pp. 152–3). In order to 'gain the upper hand', members of a 'healthy aristocracy' do to others what they 'refrain from doing' to each other: and this is not a question of 'morality or immorality', but of the 'will to power' (p. 153). In Europe, people rejoice at the prospect of 'social conditions' that will be free of exploitation, which sounds like a 'life form' lacking 'all organic functions' (p. 153). So far from being a characteristic of 'primitive' societies, 'exploitation' belongs to 'living' things' *'fundamental nature'*, deriving from the 'true will to power', and this is 'the will to life' (p. 153). This is just a *'fact'* of all history' (p. 153).

260 There are 'two basic types' of moral code: *'master moralities* **and** *slave moralities'* (p. 153). In 'higher' cultures, attempts are made to 'mediate' between them, leading to confusion, and even to elements of the two being held by the same individual (p. 153). The two sources of 'moral value distinctions' have been the 'masterful' class, conscious of how it 'differed' from the 'mastered', and the latter, the 'slaves or dependants' (pp. 153–4). The 'masters' define 'good' in terms of the 'proud, exalted states of soul', so that, in their morality, the difference between 'good' and 'bad' is that between 'noble' and 'despicable' (p. 154). There is contempt for the 'cowardly', the **'self-disparager'**, the **'craven'**, the 'flatterer' and the 'liar': all 'aristocrats' regard the 'common people' as liars (p. 154).

Historians of morality make the mistake of starting with

the values that are 'applied to *actions*', but 'value distinctions' are ascribed first 'to *people*' (p. 154). The aristocrat sees '*himself* as determining value', such that what harms him is '**harmful per se**': he '*creates values*' (p. 154). This is a 'self-glorifying' moral code, which has 'overflowing power' and consciousness of 'wealth' in the 'foreground' (p. 154). The aristocrat will 'help the unfortunate', but from 'excess of power', not 'pity' (p. 154). He relishes his own power, particularly that 'over himself', and respects all that is 'severe and harsh' (p. 154). Such people believe, and take 'pride', in themselves, and disdain '**empathetic feelings**'; they are far 'removed' from a 'moral code' that has 'pity or altruistic behaviour' at its heart (p. 155).

The 'powerful' revere 'old age' and 'origins'; they give priority to 'ancestors', at the expense of the 'next generation' (p. 155). If those who subscribe to 'modern ideas' have different priorities, and instinctively believe in 'progress and "the future"', this proves the 'ignoble' origins of their views (p. 155). The aspect of the 'master morality' that is most at odds with 'current taste' is that duties extend only to 'our peers', and that we are entitled to treat those of 'lower rank' and foreigners as we wish: in a manner that is 'beyond good and evil' (p. 155). A 'noble morality' is characterized by the 'ability and duty' to be grateful or vengeful, within a 'circle of equals'; a 'refined concept of friendship'; and a need for 'enemies', as outlets for 'envy' and 'combativeness' (p. 155).

But what about a '*slave morality*' (p. 155)? What are the common features of the 'value judgements' of the 'oppressed', 'suffering' and 'weary' (p. 155)? 'Pessimistic' about the 'human condition', they will probably condemn humanity together with it (p. 155). They will not appreciate the 'virtues of the powerful', but will give prominence to those moral 'qualities' such as 'pity', kindness and helpfulness, which are most likely to improve the 'sufferers' existence', or enable them to endure oppression (pp. 155–6). Slave morality is one 'of utility', within which the concepts of 'good' and '*evil*' originated (p. 156). The one who arouses 'fear', through 'power and dangerousness' (in 'master morality', the 'good' person, as opposed to the 'despicable' bad one), is 'evil', while the 'good' person is '*harmless*' and 'good-natured': slave morality equates 'good' with 'stupid' (p. 156). It emphasizes the 'longing for *freedom*', while 'reverence and devotion' characterize the 'aristocratic mentality': thus, '*passionate* love' has a 'noble origin' (p. 156).

261 The 'noble person' cannot comprehend 'vanity': people trying to gain the 'good opinion' of others, which they do not 'hold' themselves, then believing it (p. 156). He will acknowledge that he may be 'wrong' about his own 'worth', but will demand that others accept the worth he attaches to himself, or will welcome their 'good opinion', because he respects and loves them; it confirms his own opinion of himself; or it is 'useful' to him (p. 157). Only studying history will convince him that a 'common person', unaccustomed to 'determining values himself', is only what his 'masters' think him '*to be*' (p. 157). Even today, the 'ordinary person' awaits, and then accepts, others' 'opinion about him', whether favourable or not, just as 'pious women' take their estimate of themselves from their **father confessors** (p. 157). With the development of a 'democratic order', the 'noble and rare impulse' to 'think well' of ourselves is commended, but this is at variance with the 'older' tendency, which, in the case of 'vanity', overpowers 'the newer' (p. 157). Vain people delight in any good opinions they hear about themselves, regardless of their 'utility' or 'truth', and instinctively accept them (pp. 157–8).

The 'slave' is in 'vain' people's 'blood' (particularly in 'women'), and it tries to '*seduce*' them into having good opinions of themselves (p. 158). It then submits to 'these opinions', as if it had not summoned them: 'vanity is an atavism' (p. 158).

262 A '*species*' comes into existence, and 'grows strong', by having to battle with '*unfavourable* conditions', whereas an overprotected one tends to develop 'variations in type' and 'monstrous vices' (p. 158). In an 'aristocratic community', such as the '**ancient Greek** *polis*' or **Venice**, the priority is to breed people capable of coexistence, on whom their fellow citizens can rely, and who are equal to the challenges of fighting 'neighbours' or rebellious subject 'peoples' (p. 158). There is awareness of the 'qualities' that make 'survival' possible, and these are called 'virtues' and cultivated (p. 158). In all its aspects, from the education of children to the 'relations' between the generations, the 'aristocratic moral code' is harsh and 'intolerant': indeed, 'intolerance' is accounted a virtue, and called 'justice' (p. 158). Such a species is 'warlike, prudently **taciturn**' and 'uncommunicative' (p. 159).

Then, perhaps because its 'neighbours' are no longer hostile and there is material prosperity, the 'old discipline' is broken, or endures as a 'kind of *luxury*' (p. 159). At these '**historical turning points**', 'wild egoisms' conflict with each other, as they are unable to accept any of the 'earlier moral' code's 'limits' and restraints (p. 159). Its restrictions 'tensed the bow so ominously'; the danger 'point' is reached, when the new, 'more differentiated, richer life' outlasts the 'old morality' (p. 159). There are no 'common formulae', the 'individual' must be 'his own lawgiver', and 'misunderstanding', 'mistrust', 'decline, decay' and the 'greatest aspirations' pour forth from the 'horns of plenty' (p. 159). 'Danger' is the 'mother of morality', but what will the 'moral philosophers' of this age find to 'preach about' (pp. 159–60)? They will see everything 'going downhill' and decaying, bar one type of 'human

being': the 'incurably *mediocre*' (p. 160). They are the 'future',
the 'only survivors' (p. 160). Being mediocre will be the 'only
moral code' that 'makes sense', but it must disguise itself as
'proportion', 'dignity', 'duty' and 'brotherly love' (p. 160).

263 *'Instinct for rank'* is the clearest 'sign of *high* rank',
while *'joy'* in 'reverence' indicates 'noble origin' (p. 160). A
soul's 'greatness' is 'dangerously tested', when it comes across
something of 'the first rank', but is not protected by 'awe'
from 'intrusive poking' (p. 160). One who wishes to determine souls' 'value' and 'hierarchical position' will test their
'instinct for reverence' (p. 160). Sometimes, there is a 'quiet-
ing of all gestures', when a soul is aware of the 'proximity'
of something that is very 'worthy of reverence' (p. 160). The
continuing reverence for 'the *Bible*' may be the 'best part' of
the 'refinement in manners' that Christianity has given to
Europe (pp. 160–1). The protection that 'tyrannical external
authority' affords books of such 'depth and ultimate significance' enables them to endure long enough to be explored
and understood (p. 161). It is a huge achievement when the
'great crowd' has been 'trained' to recognize that it must treat
'holy experiences' with respect (p. 161). In contrast, what is
most obnoxious about 'so-called educated people' today is
their inability to keep their 'hands' off anything (p. 161). Perhaps, there is now 'more nobility' among the 'peasants' than
the 'newspaper-reading, intellectual *demi-monde*' (p. 161).

264 Whether a person's 'ancestors' were 'modest and
bourgeois in their desires', were accustomed to 'commanding
from dawn to dusk', or gave up 'privileges of birth and property' for the sake of 'their beliefs', it is impossible to remove
from his 'soul' the 'qualities and preferences' of a person's
'ancestors' (p. 161). This is a problem of race: 'repellent intemperance', 'narrow envy', or 'clumsy self-righteousness' will,

like 'corrupted blood', all be transmitted 'to the child' (p. 161). All 'upbringing or education' can do is *'deceive'* others about this 'inheritance' (p. 161). And, in this 'rabble-like age', this is the purpose of both: there is no room for an 'educator', who teaches 'truthfulness', and urges his 'charges' to be 'genuine' and 'natural' (p. 162).

265 'Egoism', the firm 'belief' that others must submit to us, is in the 'nature of noble souls'; it is 'in the primeval law of things' (p. 162). The 'noble soul' acknowledges that there are others with the same 'entitlements', and then, having settled the 'question of rank', interacts with these 'equals' with the 'modesty' and 'reverence' it shows to itself (p. 162). In prac- tising this 'subtle self-limitation', and yielding their 'rights' to its 'equals', it 'reveres *itself*': 'mutual reverence and rights' are the *'essence* of all society' and 'part of the natural state of things' (p. 162). 'Mercy' has no 'meaning ***inter pares***' (p. 162). Perhaps, we can be 'showered' with 'gifts from above': but the 'noble soul' is not 'adept' in such 'arts' (p. 162). It prefers to look *'ahead'*, or 'downwards': *'it knows that it is above'* (p. 162).

266 Goethe said that the only person that can be respected is one who does not seek 'himself' (p. 163).

267 The basic 'tendency' of 'contemporary' civilizations is that we 'make ourselves small': which would be the 'first thing' an 'ancient Greek' would notice (p. 163).

268 What is 'commonness' (p. 163)? For there to be 'mutual understanding', we need to have 'experiences in *com- mon*', which is why a 'single people' understand each other better than 'different peoples', even if they speak the 'same language' (p. 163). Through sharing 'experiences', they under- stand each other 'quickly'; and this is essential when there is 'danger' (p. 163). If 'the same words' have different effects on people, this can drive them apart (p. 163). The 'groups of sensations', which 'most quickly' come alive, determine the 'soul's values' and its '**table of goods**' (p. 164). If we take it that 'necessity' always brings together those who could 'indicate' similar 'needs' by similar 'signs', 'easy *communicability of necessity*' must be the most powerful force controlling 'humans' (p. 164). The 'more similar, the more common' people are (p. 164). Those who are 'select, subtle, rare' perish in 'isolation': we must resist the multiplication of 'ordinary, average, herd-like – *common*' people (p. 164).

269 If a 'psychologist' deals with 'select cases and people', he may suffocate with 'pity', and require 'cheerfulness' more than others, because, as a rule, 'differently' constituted souls 'come to ruin' (p. 164). Thus, the psychologist prefers the 'company' of 'everyday' people, for he needs a 'refuge' from 'his insights and incisions' (pp. 164–5). Sometimes, the cases that have aroused his greatest 'pity' may be those that inspire 'the crowd' with 'great reverence', as they regard them as 'great men' (p. 165). Perhaps, this is what always happens. The crowd love 'a god', but he is just a 'poor sacrificial animal' (p. 165). Indeed, 'success' is the 'biggest liar': great statesmen, conquerors, philosophers and so on are 'disguised' by their 'creations' (p. 165). Great poets like **Byron**, **Poe** or **Gogol** are 'people of the moment', 'childish, frivolous', trying to find, in their 'flights of fancy', 'oblivion' from 'all-too-faithful' memories, and feeding on 'faith itself' from their 'intoxicated' flatterers' hands (p. 165). Women like to aim their 'devoted *pity*' at them, wanting to believe that 'love can do *anything*'; but one who knows 'the heart' truly is aware of how even the 'best' love is more 'destructive than redemptive' (p. 166).

Perhaps, underneath the 'holy tale and camouflage' that is **Jesus**' life, there is the story of one who never 'had enough of any human love', and who was forced to 'invent hell', so as to send the people who 'did not *want* to love him' there; and who then had to 'invent a God who was all love', and who could pity 'human love' as 'so very paltry' (p. 166). One with that kind of knowledge of love '*seeks* death' (p. 166).

270 The 'spiritual arrogance and loathing' of one who has 'suffered deeply', and who, because he has entered 'frightful worlds' with which they are unacquainted '*knows more*' than 'most clever people', needs every form 'of disguise' to 'protect' him from 'intrusive or pitying hands' and 'everything' that is not 'equal in pain' (pp. 166–7). We are made 'noble', and separated, by 'deep suffering' (p. 167). Such camouflages include '**epicureanism**', which 'treats suffering casually'; 'cheerfulness', which gives people a 'cheerful aspect'; being 'free, impertinent spirits', who conceal 'proud, shattered, irreparable' hearts; and 'folly', which disguises 'wretched, all-too-certain knowledge' (p. 167). A 'more subtle humanity' respects 'the mask', and does not 'pursue psychology' in the 'wrong place' (p. 167).

Overview

The following section is a chapter-by-chapter overview of Friedrich Nietzsche's *Beyond Good and Evil*, designed for quick reference to the Detailed Summary above. Readers may also find this section helpful for revision.

Preface (pp. 3–4)

If truth is a woman, philosophers, as dogmatists, have failed to charm her, and dogmatism is said to be defeated. There is also reason to hope that this type of philosophy was just the infantile high-mindedness of the beginner, proving the theory that great things first appear as monstrous caricatures of themselves, like Plato's doctrines of the pure spirit and transcendental goodness. But it looks as if this error has been overcome, and the nightmare is almost over. In Europe, the battle against Plato, in the form of the Christian Church's influence, has built up a splendid tension of the spirit, which will enable us to aim at very remote targets. Many Europeans have found this tension distressing, and have tried to escape it, but those of us who are good Europeans and very free spirits feel all the distress of the spirit and the tension of the bow, and also have an arrow and a target.

Section 1
On the Prejudices of Philosophers (pp. 5–24)

1 Nietzsche asks what sort of questions the will to truth presents to philosophers, and what impels them to get at the truth. Much time is spent questioning the will's origin, and

value, but why are untruth, uncertainty or ignorance not preferable? It is as if the problem has never been posed. Now we are daring to face it, and no daring is greater.

2 It is held to be impossible for something to originate in its opposite, for example, truth in error. Things with the highest value have their own origin, which cannot be the perishable or lowly. But this is the metaphysicians' characteristic prejudice, driving them to seek their 'knowledge', which they then call 'the truth'. They claim to doubt everything, but not the opposition of values, and do not consider that these opposites and value judgements might be temporary perspectives. Truth and altruism are highly valued, but perhaps appearance, the will to illusion, egoism and desire should be, too. A new breed of philosophers of the dangerous 'Perhaps' is awaited.

3 Most conscious thinking, including philosophical, is instinctive, so a fresh understanding of heredity and the innate are required. Value judgements, specifically the physiological imperative to preserve a particular kind of life, as in the views that certainty and truth are more valuable than uncertainty and appearance, underlie all logic. But, unless man is the measure of everything, these may be mere foreground evaluations, necessary to preserve beings like us.

4 Our interest is not in a judgement's truth or falsity, but its tendency to preserve life and the species. The most false judgements, synthetic *a priori* ones, are regarded as the most indispensable. We believe we could not survive without logical fictions and mathematical falsifications of the world. Accepting untruth as a condition of life means resisting familiar values in a dangerous way, and a philosophy that dares to do so puts itself beyond good and evil.

5 It is philosophers' lack of honesty, not their guilelessness or childishness, that makes us distrust them. They profess to reach their opinions by independently unravelling a cold, pure dialectic, but actually, in a cunning way, find reasons to justify a pre-existing view, and put forward an abstract version of their greatest desires and the prejudices they call truths. Kant is hypocritical, enticing us down dialectical backroads to his categorical imperative, and Spinoza seems timid and assailable, cloaking his philosophy in the hocus-pocus of mathematical form, to protect it from critics.

6 Every great philosophy is its author's personal confession, originating from the moral, or immoral, aims in it. When he tries to explain the most far-fetched metaphysical propositions, we need to ask about the philosopher's own morality. Instinct for knowledge is not the origin of philosophy; rather, a different instinct has made knowledge its tool. Indeed, every human instinct practises philosophy, as it wants to present itself as existence's ultimate aim and the master of all the others. All our instincts are tyrannical and seek to philosophize. Truly scientific people's instinct for knowledge may operate without engaging the other instincts. And it does not matter to which area of science they apply it; it is not their specialist area that marks them out. There is nothing impersonal about the philosopher: his morality determines who he is and how his innermost drives are organized.

7 Philosophers can be malicious. Epicurus suggested that Plato and his followers lacked genuineness. He resented their grandiosity and theatricality. He hid away, and wrote hundreds of books; it took Greece a hundred years to appreciate who he was.

8 Every philosophical work features the philosopher's convictions.

9 The Stoics' exhortation to live according to nature is deceitful. It would be wasteful, and lacking in purpose, conscience, compassion and fairness to do so. Living involves preferring, wanting to be different, and wishing to be other than nature. But, if living according to nature means only according to life, we cannot do otherwise. Those who profess this have a very different aim: to dictate their morality and ideals to nature, and to refashion it according to Stoicism. They gaze endlessly at nature, but see it distortedly, from their own perspective. They then cling to the mad hope that, as they can tyrannize themselves, they can do so with nature. What happened during the Stoic era is always repeated, once philosophy starts to believe in itself. Philosophy is the most spiritual form of the will to power, and shapes the world in its own image.

10 Europe today endlessly discusses the issue of the real and apparent world, but this does not indicate a will to truth. A few puritanical fanatics may prefer certainty of 'Nothing' to an uncertain 'Something', but this is nihilism, revealing despair and spiritual exhaustion. More energetic thinkers take a stand against appearance, and seem willing to give up their bodies, their surest possession. Perhaps, their root desire is to regain what was once possessed even more certainly, and which produced a better life than modern ideas: the immortal soul or the old God. Modern ideas are distrusted, and current positivism held in contempt. Today's sceptical anti-realists see no reason to resist their desire to escape modern reality, but, if they were stronger, they would want to go beyond, not back.

11 Kant's real influence on German philosophy is missed. He was proudest of his table of categories, but what he really took pride in was discovering a new human faculty, that of making synthetic *a priori* judgements. German philosophy's flowering stemmed from his disciples competing to make an equally significant discovery. But Kant's actual achievement was to conclude that a faculty made possible synthetic *a priori*

judgements; and even greater rejoicing followed his discovery of a moral faculty. The young theologians searched for others, and found one for the extra-sensual, that of intellectual intuition. But saying a faculty makes something possible explains nothing; it just repeats the question. Kant's question about the possibility of synthetic *a priori* judgements must be countered by asking why we need to believe in them. It is because, though possibly false, their truth has to be accepted, to preserve creatures like us: it is a foreground belief. People welcomed German philosophy's antidote to the sensualism pouring from the eighteenth into the nineteenth century.

12 Boscovich and Copernicus successfully challenged belief in the appearance of things, ending our belief in substance, and convincing us that the earth does not stand still. But, the battle against the persisting atomistic need must go on, starting with Christianity's: that the soul is ineradicable, eternal and indivisible. This does not mean dispensing with one of our oldest hypotheses, but revised versions of it are needed, like the mortal soul, or the soul as the social construct of drives and emotions. Thus, science can drive out the superstitions clustering around the idea of the soul.

13 Living beings want to release their strength; life is will to power. Physiologists should look again at the view that self-preservation is the primary instinct. We must beware of such superfluous teleological principles.

14 A few thinkers see that physics is a way of interpreting, not explaining, the world; but its reliance on belief in the senses makes it seem something more. The strength of Plato's approach is that it resists belief in the senses, and imposes a structure of concepts on the confused information we receive through them. Plato's interpretation of the world differs from that of the physicists, including Darwinists and

anti-teleologists. Their principle, that human beings have nothing more to seek, if they have nothing else to see and grasp, is very different from his.

15 Conscientious practice of physiology involves not regarding the sense organs as phenomena in the philosophical idealist sense; they could not then be causes. Some argue that the sense organs create the external world, but this would mean they created our bodies, too, which is absurd.

16 Some philosophers believe in immediate certainties, such as 'I think' or 'I will', as if perception can grasp things in themselves. Popular belief notwithstanding, the philosopher must recognize that the proposition, 'I think', involves unprovable assertions, such as that 'I' am the thinking one; that an 'I' exists; and so on. Again, the reference back to previous states in 'I think' indicates a lack of immediate certainty. Philosophers face a series of metaphysical questions about the origin of the concept of thinking; the reasons for belief in cause and effect; and the right to talk about an 'I'. Today's philosophers will challenge attempts to answer these questions by invoking some sort of intellectual intuition, as in claiming that 'I think' is true, real and certain.

17 Logicians hate to admit that a thought comes when it wishes, not when 'I' do. It falsifies the facts to state that 'I' is the condition of the predicate 'think'. The 'I' is a hypothesis, not an immediate certainty, and even to say there is thinking involves interpretation. The reasoning process is that thinking is an activity; for each activity, there is someone who acts; and so on.

18 The theory of free will has often been refuted, but endures for this reason.

19 Philosophers like Schopenhauer talk as if the whole world knows about the will, but willing only has unity as a word. The act involves an inseparable commanding thought and an emotion. So-called freedom of the will is the emotion of superiority to the one obeying. Willing involves concentration on what must be had, and inner certainty of obedience: one who wills commands something within himself, which obeys, or which he believes will. We obey, as well as command, and experience coercion and resistance after the act of will; but, through the synthetic concept 'I', overlook this division. We believe willing is enough for action, and, because we expect obedience, regard the effect as necessary, so will and action are one. Free will refers to the complex pleasurable condition of the person willing, who both commands, and carries out the command. This is what happens in well-structured, happy communities, where the ruling class identifies with its success. Willing is commanding and obeying, and the philosopher can understand it from within ethics, which is the theory of hierarchical relationships, from which life originates.

20 Philosophical concepts do not just appear, but develop in relation to one another. However independent of, or different from, each other they seem, they follow one another in a certain order. Philosophizing is high order atavism: concepts are recognized and remembered afresh. Where there is linguistic affinity, similar philosophical developments occur, while other ways of interpreting the world are ruled out. Locke's superficiality about the origin of ideas must be rejected.

21 Being one's own cause is a contradictory idea, which is hard to resist, due to excessive human pride. Another form of it is longing for free will, so that we can be wholly responsible for our actions. We should rid ourselves of this non-concept and its opposite, the unfree will. Our error is not appreciating

that cause and effect are conventional fictions, which describe, but do not explain. We invented causes, freedom and reason, and it is a myth to think they are signs of what the world is in itself. In real life, there is no unfree will, only strong and weak ones. Detecting coercion or constraint in a causal connection indicates one's own inadequacy. Constraint of the will is always treated as a personal problem, whether by those with self-belief, who want credit for everything, or by those whose self-contempt impels them to deny responsibility. When weak-willed people write books, they often adopt socialistic compassion, and their fatalism looks better as a religion of suffering humanity.

22 As an old philologist, I must point out the bad interpretative practice of physicists talking about nature's lawfulness. It is not a fact, but a naive humanitarian interpretation, enabling current democratic instincts to be accommodated: as there is so much equality before the law, it must be in nature, too. But an equally convincing interpretation of natural phenomena is as the relentlessly unmerciful assertion of power, of the will to power. This interpretation can also claim that the world is necessary and predictable, not because laws operate in it, but because there are none.

23 Up to now, moral prejudices and fears have held back psychology, so I am the only one to approach these matters as a study of the will to power. A true physio-psychology must overcome the researcher's conscience, which is offended by a theory that good and bad instincts are conditions of each other and that the former derive from the latter. But hatred, envy, greed, power-hunger are fundamental to life, and must be intensified, if life is going to be. We are going to journey beyond morality, and may crush what is left in the process. But there have been no deeper insights, and the psychologist,

who makes this sort of sacrifice, may insist on psychology being acknowledged as the queen of the sciences.

Section 2
The Free Spirit (pp. 25–42)

24 We have clung to ignorance, to lead free, thoughtless and careless lives. We could only base our science on such ignorance while the basis of our will to knowledge is lack of it, uncertainty and untruth. And, even though we who know discover that deep-seated moral hypocrisy distorts our words, occasionally we grasp what has happened, and laugh at how even the best science loves error, and imprisons us in this neatly falsified world.

25 Philosophers must not defend themselves or be martyrs, as they will spoil their consciences' objectivity, and make themselves stupid and brutish, through fighting accusations. They do not need to defend truth on earth, as if it needed defenders. It does not matter whether they are proved right: no philosopher has been. They should keep out of the way. Lengthy wars which cannot be fought openly make people venomous and bad. In spite of spiritual disguises, the long-term fugitives and enforced hermits, like Spinoza and Bruno, turn into elegant avengers and poisoners. Foolish moral indignation marks out a philosopher who has lost his philosophical humour. The philosopher's sacrifice for truth brings out the propagandist and the actor in him. People have seen him as just an artistic curiosity, but now want to see him in his degeneracy. It is a question whether this will prove that the long tragedy (assuming every philosophy, as it takes shape, is one) is over.

26 An exceptional person seeks refuge from the general run of humanity, but one factor impels him towards it: interaction with others may cause distress, but evading it means he is not equipped for knowledge. He must set aside good taste, recognizing that the rule is more interesting than the exception. Studying the average man is a serious, if unpleasant, activity, which is essential for every philosopher. He may encounter so-called cynics, who will make his task easier: they recognize what is common (the rule they live by), but are willing to discuss it openly. Cynicism is the form in which common souls approach honesty: we find an exceptional mind with a common heart. The lover of knowledge must listen attentively when someone talks critically, but not indignantly, about humans, as if their only motives are hunger, sexual desire and vanity. In moral terms, indignant people may rank above the self-satisfied and lustful, but are more common and less instructive.

27 Life among those who live as frogs makes it hard to be understood, so we are indebted to the subtle interpreters. But, good friends are too comfortable, so we should allow them space for misunderstanding. This will give amusement, and we may be able to dispense with them entirely, which will also be amusing.

28 It is hard to translate the tempo of one language's style into another, and some well-meant translations just make the original crude. This is a problem for Germans, who cannot manage the nuances of free-spirited thought in Aristophanes and Petronius. Germans, even Goethe, tend to be solemn and clumsy. Lessing is better. He translated Bayle, enjoyed Diderot and Voltaire, and adored freethinking and escaping Germany; but even he could not match Machiavelli. No one would attempt to translate Petronius or Aristophanes into German. Plato had a copy of the latter's work under his deathbed: even he could not have endured life without it.

29 Only a few strong people can be independent, and, when one who does not need to be attempts it, he is probably recklessly bold. As no one sees him going astray, he is likely to perish; he is so far away from human understanding that they do not feel it, or for him.

30 Our loftiest insights seem foolish to those not equipped to hear them. Whereas the easily intelligible philosopher makes judgements from the outside and below, the profound one does so from above. The soul can attain heights from which even tragedy no longer has a tragic effect, so it is hard to determine whether it should elicit particular pity. An ordinary man's virtues might be a philosopher's vices. Books exist whose value depends on whether they are used by lower or higher forms of human life: with the former, they are dangerous, with the latter, calls to valour. An odour of small people clings to common people's books, eating-places and even places of worship.

31 When young, we indulge and abuse our taste for the unconditional. Habitually angry and awe-struck youth falsifies people and things, so as to vent their feelings on them. After the torture of endless disappointments, young souls turn in on themselves, and tear themselves apart, as if they had chosen delusion. Then we distrust our feelings; feel our good conscience is a danger, masking our finer honesty; and take sides against youth. Ten years later, we see that the whole process was youth.

32 In the prehistoric age, consequences decided an action's value. This was a pre-moral period, when no one was aware of the importance of knowing oneself. Since then, we have learned to determine an action's value by its origins. This was the moral period, indicating an effort at self-knowledge. But a new superstition came with the change: narrow interpretation of origin as intention. So, there was agreement that an action's value lay in the value of its intention.

This might be the dawn of the extra-moral age. We immoralists suspect that an action's conscious part is like a skin, hiding not revealing, and that its non-intentional part shows its value. We think intentions need interpretation, and that intention-morality is a prejudice, to be overcome. The self-overcoming of morality is a task reserved for today's most subtle and honest, if malicious, people of conscience.

33 We must closely examine our feelings of devotion, sacrifice for our neighbour, the morality of self-renunciation and disinterested contemplation. The feelings that surround doing things for others' sake, not one's own, sound like seductions. We may like them, but this is not an argument for them. We must be careful.

34 Whatever our philosophical viewpoint, the erroneous nature of the world strikes us; we may think there is something deceptive in the nature of things. But, if we think that this is due to our thought processes, and that we infer the world falsely, we would have good reason to doubt them. There is something touching in the innocence of thinkers who demand honest answers from their consciousness, such as why it keeps the outside world at such a distance. But philosophers' faith in immediate certainties is stupid. It may be that, in bourgeois life, distrust is regarded as indicating bad character, but, today, the philosopher's duty is to be distrustful.

I now take a different view of deception. Valuing truth as more than appearance is moral prejudice. There would be no life or truth without appearances. The question is why we must accept an essential difference between truth and falsity, rather than degrees of appearance. The world that is relevant to us could be fictitious, as could any question about its author.

35 Truth and searching for it are not trivial matters. Going about the latter in too human a manner will mean not finding anything.

36 If we are given nothing real, except our world of desires and passions, and the only reality is that of our instincts, this could explain the material world as one with the same level of reality as emotion: a rudimentary form of the world of emotions, which holds the potential of the organic process in a powerful unity, and in which all the organic functions are synthetically linked.

The conscience of our method requires us to conduct such an experiment. We must not conclude that there are several types of causality, until certain that only one is not enough. The question we face is whether we accept the causality of the will, and whether this is the only one. Wills can only affect other wills, not matter, so our hypothesis is that, wherever there are effects, one will is affecting another, and that all mechanical events are actually effects of the will. If our instinctive and organic life and functions could be explained as the development of one basic form of the will, the will to power, and this enabled us to solve the problem of procreation and alimentation, we could describe all effective energy as the will to power, which would describe the world by its intelligible character.

37 This does not mean that God has been disproved, but not the devil.

38 Commentators have projected their own feelings on to that gruesome and unnecessary farce, the French Revolution, for so long that the actual events have vanished under the interpretation. Posterity could do this to the whole of history, to make it seem bearable. It may have happened already. As we realize this, we may be able to stop it.

39 Nobody thinks a doctrine is true just because it makes us happy or virtuous; but this does not mean what makes us unhappy or evil is false. A harmful and dangerous thing, which it might destroy us to understand, could still be true. A person's strength of spirit might be gauged by his capacity for tolerating the undisguised truth. Wicked people are better at discovering aspects of the truth, and, though moralists say nothing about them, there are happy wicked people. Harshness and cunning may favour development of strength and independence of spirit more than the accommodating good nature we value in scholars: assuming we do not limit the concept of philosopher to writers of books. Stendhal said a good philosopher should be dry, clear and illusion-free, having something of a banker's character.

40 Deep things love a mask. Some experiences are so delicate that they should be concealed as a coarse act. Some people know how to abuse their own memories, to take revenge on this one confidant. It is not the worst things that make us most ashamed. It is not only wicked cunning behind a mask; there is so much kindness in cunning. One who is deeply ashamed will hide his mortal danger from his neighbours and friends. Such a secretive one asks that, in his place, a mask inhabits his friends' hearts and minds. Every deep spirit requires a mask; and one is continually growing there anyway, due to the shallow interpretations of everything he says and does.

41 Those of us destined to command must test ourselves, and not try to avoid it, though we are the only judge. We must not depend on anyone, a fatherland, pity, science, or even our own detachment. We must not rely on our own virtues, nor sacrifice our wholeness to one of our singular qualities, such as being liberal, until it becomes a vice. We must learn how to preserve ourselves, the greatest test of independence.

42 A new breed of philosophers is coming, and, though they wish to remain a riddle, they will be experimenters; but the very term is an experiment and temptation.

43 These new philosophers will probably be new friends of truth. They will not be dogmatists, as it would be against their pride to impose truth on others. We must free ourselves from the bad taste of wanting to agree with a lot of other people. As for common goods, it is a contradiction, for what is common lacks value. Ultimately, things must stay as they are. The great will keep the great things, the depths are for the profound, while everything extraordinary remains with the extraordinary.

44 These philosophers of the future will be very free spirits, and something greater. However, the term 'free spirit' must not be misunderstood. In Europe and America, there are false free spirits, prolific scribblers who promote democratic tastes and modern ideas. They are not free spirits, and are superficial, ascribing all human misery to failure of society's structures. Their slogans are 'equal rights' and 'compassion for all suffering'; they are trying to create a happy world for the masses.

But, we know that human beings flourish under the opposite conditions, and that pressure and discipline improve the human spirit, intensifying it into unconditional power-will. The evil, frightful and tyrannical elevate human beings. These views are the antithesis of all modern ideology. As free spirits, we do not communicate, having no desire to disclose what a spirit can free itself from, or be driven to. The dangerous phrase, 'beyond good and evil', prevents misidentification as modern freethinkers. We hate the temptations to dependence that lurk in honours, money, position or sensory enthusiasms, and are indebted to distress and illness, which free us from the common rule and its prejudice. Our surplus of free will prepares us for every adventure, while nobody can readily discern our ultimate intentions. We are friends of solitude and free spirits. The new philosophers have something of this.

Section 3
The Religious Disposition (pp. 43–57)

45 A born psychologist searches for the human soul's boundaries and the inner life's dimensions. He also feels that he is on his own, and longs for, but has difficulty finding, helpers. It is pointless sending scholars into such dangerous hunting grounds, for they lose their eye. To grasp the history of such a problem as awareness and conscience in religious people's souls would probably require Pascal's monstrous intellectual conscience. Suitable helpers may never appear, so, if you want to know something, you must do it yourself. Curiosity like mine is a pleasant vice; or rather love of truth brings its own heavenly and earthly rewards.

46 Early Christian faith, in a world of different philosophical schools, taught tolerance by the Romans, was not like Luther and Cromwell's naive and quarrelsome faith. From the start, Christianity has demanded sacrifice of freedom and pride, and subjugation and self-derision, while assuming the indescribable pain of spiritual submission. Today, we are deadened to Christian language, and do not appreciate the significance of the formula 'God on the Cross', which produced a re-evaluation of ancient values. The slaves avenged themselves on Rome's noble but frivolous tolerance: their masters' smiling indifference to the seriousness of faith inflamed them, and made them rebel. Enlightenment infuriates the slave; even in morality, he grasps only the tyrannical, and rages against the aristocrat's noble sensibility, which appears to deny suffering. This scepticism about suffering was a major cause of the last great slave rebellion, which started with the French Revolution.

47 Solitude, fasting and sexual abstinence always accompany the religious neurosis, though extravagant voluptuousness, followed by penitence and denial of the world, is another symptom. Nothing else has produced so much nonsense and superstition, and drawn so much interest, even from philosophers. Underlying recent philosophy like Schopenhauer's is the issue of religious crisis and awakening, of the possibility of denying the will, and of sainthood. The Salvation Army is the latest manifestation of the religious neurosis, available for psychiatric investigation. The phenomenon of the saint fascinates philosophers, as it involves opposite conditions of the soul with opposite moral values: a bad person could become good. But earlier psychology made the mistake of believing in moral value oppositions, and reading them into the case.

48 Roman Catholicism is more internalized among the Latin races than any type of Protestantism is among northern Europeans. In Roman Catholic countries, not having faith is to rebel against the race's spirit; but, reflecting our barbarian origins, for us northerners it means returning to it. The French, having some Celtic blood, produce even pious sceptics, like Comte, Saint-Beuve and Renan. Renan's idea, that religion is produced by a normal person, who is most right when most religious and assured of infinite life, is alien to my way of thinking.

49 The ancient Greeks' religious attitude was characterized by great gratitude, and only noble people can face nature thus. The rabble then gained control, and fear entered religion, preparing the way for Christianity.

50 Luther's passion for God, that of an undeservedly pardoned slave, is, like Augustine's, boorish, naive and lacking in nobility.

51 Powerful people respect the saint as a riddle of self-discipline and ultimate renunciation, sensing a superior force behind his pitiable appearance. By honouring him, they honoured something in themselves, yet they suspected an underlying reason for so great a denial: that a great danger existed, of which the ascetic was aware. Around him, the powerful of the world became conscious of a new, unconquered enemy: the will to power.

52 Nothing in Greek or Indian literature compares to the Old Testament. It connects us with the tremendous remnants of what humanity used to be. A touchstone of greatness or smallness, it will not affect tame house-pets, like today's civilized Christians, whose taste is for the New Testament, which reeks of devotees and small souls. It has been joined with the Old Testament into the Bible, which is literary Europe's greatest sin against the spirit.

53 Atheism now prevails, because God does not hear, or communicate clearly. In Europe, the religious instinct grows strongly, but is not satisfied by theism.

54 Since Descartes, philosophers have tried to destroy the old concept of the soul. Epistemological scepticism is anti-Christian, though not anti-religious. Previously, people instinctively believed in the soul, holding that 'I' is a condition, and 'think' a conditioned predicate. Then they wondered if the reverse might be the case, and 'I' a synthesis, made through thinking itself. Kant wished to prove that neither subject nor object could not be proved by means of the subject. He may have been aware of the subject or soul's apparent existence, an idea present in the philosophy of Vedanta.

55 There are three very significant aspects of religious cruelty. In ancient times, people sacrificed human beings to their gods; then, as they developed morally, their strongest instincts or nature; and, finally (reserved for this generation), the only thing left to sacrifice: God, the source of future bliss and justice; and all for the sake of nothingness.

56 One who must struggle to think down to the depths of pessimism, and save it from its half-Christian, half-German narrowness of expression in Schopenhauer's philosophy, and who looks into the most world-denying of all ways of thinking, that which is beyond good and evil, and not deluded by morality, will see the opposite ideal: that of a lively, world-affirming human being, who accepts it, and wishes to have it over again, just as it was and is, through eternity.

57 As a human being's intellectual sight and insight grow stronger, the space surrounding him increases, and he comes across new images and riddles. Ultimately, everything, including the most solemn concepts of God and sin, may seem no more important than childhood toys to an old man.

58 A truly religious life of detailed self-examination and prayer, to prepare for God's coming, demands leisure, so differs little from the aristocratic view that work debases soul and body. Our present-day work ethic acclimatizes us to lack of faith, and destroys any idea of the possible use of religion. Apart from theologians, people today have too much to do to spare time for religion. They are not antagonistic to religious customs, but are too remote from them to have views about them. Today's German scholar finds it hard to take religion

seriously. Even if historical study has made him grateful to religion, indifference makes him avoid religious people or things, while his tolerance of them is accompanied by a sense of distress. His faith in his own superiority is naive, as he is a presumptuous little vulgarian, producing modern ideas.

59 Our instinct for preservation makes us light and false. Perhaps, the born artists, whose sole pleasure seems to be falsification of life's image, belong to a hierarchy, and their degree of sickness of life can be gauged by the extent of their desire to adulterate its image. The religious people among the artists are those of the highest class. For thousands of years, people's incurable pessimism has compelled them to hold on to a religious interpretation of existence. So, piety seems to be an exquisite result of fear of the truth. It may be that piety is the most powerful device for beautifying human beings, as it can make them so completely into art that there is no suffering involved in looking at them.

60 Loving mankind for God's sake is human beings' most noble and far-fetched feeling: that, without an ulterior motive, loving people is just another brutish stupidity. Whoever first thought this should be venerated as one who has erred beautifully.

61 As free spirits, we see the philosopher as one whose conscience includes human beings' overall development, and who will use religions as he does political and economic circumstances, to improve education and breeding. For the strong and independent, religion is another way of surmounting obstacles and learning to rule. It ties rulers and ruled together, handing over to the first the second's consciences and innermost secret, the desire to be free of having to obey. If, from higher spirituality, some prefer a contemplative life, religions can afford them respite from the cruder type of authority, and purity, when facing the inevitable filth of political activity. This is what the Brahmans did, appointing kings, but staying outside the political process.

Religion tests the self-control and solitude of those among the governed, who wish to be leaders, and guides them. Asceticism and puritanism are indispensable means of educating and improving a race that wants to overcome its origin in the rabble. It also makes those who serve and are useful content, by justifying their everyday lives. Its effect is the same as Epicurean philosophy's on higher-class sufferers: it purifies and sanctifies suffering. Perhaps, Christianity and Buddhism's most admirable aspect is teaching the lowliest people that piety gives them a position in an illusory higher order of things, thus reconciling them to the real order and their harsh lives.

62 There is danger when religions hold sway, not as the philosopher intends, as a means for education, but as ultimate ends. Humanity has a surplus of degenerate and suffering people, and the law of meaninglessness is most destructive to higher individuals, whose needs are hard to identify. The two greatest religions regard themselves as religions for the suffering, treating those who suffer from life as being in the right. Their solicitude is admirable, but they tend to preserve too much of what should perish. We are indebted to Christians for what they have done for Europe, but by the time they have comforted the suffering, and supported the dependent, the only other thing they could do to ensure the European race's degeneration is to twist all that is masculine, triumphant, tyrannical – love of earthly things and of being the earth's master – into hatred of the earth and the earthly. Christianity's history in Europe shows that one will, intent on making humanity into a sublime deformity, prevails. A god, looking at the capriciously degenerate being that is the

European Christian, might protest angrily at the way his most beautiful stone has been hacked and ruined.

Christianity has enabled people who were neither strong nor far-sighted, and who cannot accept that there is a gulf between human and human, to control Europe's destiny, and, with their insistence that people are equal in the eyes of God, to breed a sickly and mediocre species, today's European.

Section 5
Towards a Natural History of Morals (pp. 74–92)

186 Europe's current moral sensitivity is as subtle and mature as the science of morality is raw and crude: a contrast sometimes found in the moralist. We must appreciate our long-term needs, and gather the material for a complete classification of morals. Thus far, there is a lack of modesty. Philosophers used to be interested in morality as a science. They tried to explain morality, and think they have done so. But clumsy pride has left them a long way from the apparently modest, but essential, task of description. Moral philosophers knew the facts of morality only roughly, as that of their class or Church. Ill informed about peoples and history, they did not grasp the real problems of morality, which only become apparent by comparing many moral systems. What they thought was an explanation of morality was no more than a learned form of true belief in current morality, or a new way of expressing it, and so was part of the situation within it. It was the opposite of analysing and doubting their particular moral views. So Schopenhauer claims that all moralists agree that harming no one, and helping everyone as much as possible, is the foundation of morality and the moral principle they try to account for.

He could not account for it, and it is a false and sentimental principle in a world whose essence is the will to power. We should also ask of Schopenhauer whether a pessimist, who denies God and the world, but stops short at the problem of morality, accepts a harm-no-one morality, and who plays the flute, really is a pessimist.

187 As well as asking about their value, we can also ask what an assertion, like 'a categorical imperative exists within us', says about the one who asserts it. Moral codes are meant to justify their author to others, to nail him to the cross, to enable the moralist to exercise his power and creative whims on others, and so on. In his code, Kant declares that what is honourable about him is his ability to obey, and it should be the same for everybody. So, moral codes are just sign languages of emotions.

188 Every moral code that is against just letting things be exemplifies tyranny against nature and reason; but this objection would mean invoking another code, banning tyranny and unreason. The invaluable characteristic of every moral code is that it involves coercion, the way to achieve strength and freedom. Poets and orators have had to submit to tyrannical laws, but strangely, everything to do with freedom, daring and perfect sureness, whether in ideas, governance, or oratory, has developed through such laws, suggesting that they, not letting things be, are what is natural. A long period of enforced obedience seems to produce everything, such as virtue, art, reason and spirituality, which makes life worth living. Coercion; having to work within court or church guidelines; having to find God in everything: such violence and harshness may have suppressed much energy and spirit, but made the European spirit strong and curious, as thinkers knew what the result of their work had to be. Slavery seems

the indispensable means of disciplining and cultivating the spirit. All this makes us distrustful of letting things be, indicating that narrower perspectives and being stupid are preconditions of life and growth. A long period of obedience, without which self-respect will be lost, is nature's moral imperative. It is not, as Kant insisted, categorical, and is not addressed to individuals, but to human beings in general.

189 Leisure is a burden for hard-working races. Wisely, the English keep Sunday holy and humdrum, so that people want to get back to work. We need days of fasting, when powerful instincts and habits can be held in check. History reveals whole eras as times of coercion and fasting, when instincts are subdued, but also purified and intensified. This is a way to interpret the rise of a sect, like the Stoics, in a Greek culture that was rank and stale. It also explains why, in Europe's most Christian age, under the influence of its value judgements, the sexual drive was sublimated into love.

190 An alien element in Plato's morality is Socratism, which includes the argument that no one desires to do himself harm, so it happens involuntarily. The bad man would not do harm if he knew that bad was bad, and does so in error. By removing this, we make him good. This argument focuses only on a bad action's bad consequences, while the good is the useful and pleasant. Other forms of moral utilitarianism have a similar origin. Plato tried his best to make Socrates' views subtle and noble, by turning them into the infinite and impossible.

191 The theological issue of faith versus knowledge, of whether value judgements give more authority to instinct or rationality, is the old moral problem Socrates addressed, which long predates Christianity. At first, Socrates sided with reason, but then, studying his conscience, he discovered that he

was like the Athenian nobles he was mocking. He concluded
that we must follow our instincts, but persuade reason to give
it good arguments. Thus, he realized the irrational aspect of
moral judgements.

Plato sought to show that, if left alone, reason and instinct
aim at a single goal, the good or God. Since then, theologians
and philosophers have followed the same path, and instinct,
faith or the herd have triumphed in moral matters. Descartes was the exception, but reason is just a tool and he was
superficial.

192 Students of the history of science find it helps us to
understand the common processes in acquiring knowledge.
First, there are over-eager hypotheses and lack of scepticism.
Then our senses develop greater caution. We find it easier to
reproduce a familiar image than to retain what is different
and new about an impression. Our senses are averse to new
things, while the emotions tend to dominate. When reading,
people barely distinguish five words out of twenty, and we
make up most of even our strangest experiences. We are used
to lying, or, to put it less harshly, are artists more than we realize. In conversation, I see my partner's face in terms of the
thought he is expressing, or that I think I have elicited from
him, in a way that exceeds my ability to see. He was probably
making a different face, or none.

193 Our experiences in dreams are as much part of our soul
as our actual experience, and make life richer or poorer. If
someone dreams he is able to fly, this must make him happier while awake, and what the poets call soaring seem too
earthly.

194 Human diversity shows itself not only in differing
tables of goods, and disputes about their comparative value,
but in how possession of these goods is defined. A modest

man sees his sexual relationship with a woman as proof that he possesses her; a more suspicious one wants to be sure that she is giving up all she has for him. A still more distrustful man wants her to know him thoroughly, before accepting her love, so that she does not love an image of him. One man, who wishes to possess a people, adopts high political arts, but another is not satisfied that a mere image of himself should hold sway over them, preferring to be known and to know himself. Benevolent people often redraw the character of potential recipients, to make them worthy of help, and so control the needy like property. Parents educate their children to be like themselves, and subject them to their own judgements, as do teachers, classes, priests and princes.

195 The Jews, whom Tacitus thought born to slavery, but who saw themselves as the chosen people, achieved a reversal of values that made it possible for life on earth to become newly and dangerously fascinating for up to two thousand years. Their prophets combined discordant concepts into a single entity, first used the word 'world' as a curse, and treated 'poor' as a synonym for 'saint'. The slave revolt in morals began with them.

196 We can deduce that there are dark heavenly bodies near to the sun that we will never see. This is a metaphor, and the moral psychologist will read the celestial text as one, as a sign language that keeps a lot silent.

197 Moralists misunderstand predatory people and animals; they examine these healthy creatures for their diseased state. The high-spirited person is classified as degenerate, while moderate, moral and mediocre people are favoured.

198 Moral codes for individuals, aimed at their happiness, are guides, designed to counter the passions and will to power. They generalize where they should not, using unconditional language. Intellectually, this is worth little, whether it takes the form of a remedy against emotional folly, or an Aristotelian toning down of the emotions to a harmless mean. It is neither science nor wisdom, but combines shrewdness and stupidity. It might be a morality of enjoyment of emotions, diluted through art, love of God, or of mankind for God's sake. It could be wanton devotion to the emotions, a bold dropping of the reins.

199 There have always been human herds, and more followers than commanders. Human beings have practised obedience for so long that everyone is born with a need to obey. Human development has been retarded by the herd instinct to obey, at the expense of skill in commanding. Commanders are scarce, or pretend not to give commands. The moral hypocrisy they practise in Europe today is to claim that they are carrying out someone else's orders, such as those of the constitution or God, or are acting for the common good. The herd man has become self-important, parading his qualities of docility and usefulness to the herd, like true human virtues. Now, people try to replace commanders with the cleverest herd people, which is the origin of all representative constitutions. A Napoleon has a powerful effect on the European herd animals: its history is that of the greatest happiness the entire century achieved.

200 One who lives in an age of disintegration, which mixes races, will carry the heritage of his mixed origins in his own contradictory and warring standards and instincts. Essentially weak, he will want the war he embodies to end. Endorsing a tranquillizing mentality, like Christianity, he will consider happiness to be rest. But the warlike oppositions within him may stimulate him to live more, and, if he has the expertise and cunning to fight with himself, he may become one of those unfathomable men, destined for victory and seduction. Both types belong together, and arise from the same causes.

201 While moral judgements reflect the herd, and we identify immorality as what endangers communal stability, there can be no morality of neighbourly love. Tiny acts of consideration, sympathy and fairness, which in time we will describe as virtues, are present, but as yet are outside morality. In Rome's heyday, an act of pity was not good or evil, but was simply disdained in comparison to an act that could benefit the whole commonwealth. In the end, neighbourly love comes second to fear of one's neighbour. Once there is security against external threats, this is what drives value judgements. Such instincts as adventurousness and lust for power were encouraged as useful against common enemies, but now only their danger is appreciated, and they are condemned. The present moral outlook, born of the herd instinct, focuses on things that are harmful to the community and equality; so, again, fear is the mother of morality. Everything, even great powers of reason, which elevates the individual, is seen as evil. In extremely peaceful conditions, any sternness or harshness is regarded as offensive. We may reach a point when society sides with criminals, and thinks it unfair to punish them. It is the morality of herdlike timidity. We want to have nothing to fear; in today's Europe, the will for this is called progress.

202 People do not want to hear the truth, and we will be thought criminal for using a term like 'herd' of people with modern ideas. We have no choice. Today's Europeans think they know what Socrates did not: what is good and evil. But it is the herd animal that thinks it knows, and calls itself good. Europe's current morality is that of the herd animal, which vigorously defends itself against alternatives. With religion's help, we have Christianity's heir, the democratic movement, the progress of which, judging by increasingly frantic protests, is too slow for its overeager advocates. They are against every form of society other than autonomous herds, and seem to be at odds with peaceable democrats. They are hostile to every exceptional right and privilege (no one needs rights, when all are equal), and united in their religion of pity and mortal hatred of any suffering. They are committed to communal pity, as if it is morality itself, and seem to want to subject Europe to a new Buddhism. What they cling to is belief in the community as a redeemer, in the herd and in themselves.

203 Those of us who see the democratic movement as a decadent form of political organization, which makes human beings mediocre, place our hopes in the new philosophers. They will have the strength and originality to oppose current value judgements, and will take a new direction. They will lay the foundations for daring experiments in discipline and breeding, which will end the reign of nonsense and coincidence we call history, of which the preoccupation with the welfare of the greatest number is just the latest manifestation. For this, new philosophers and leaders are required who will be free spirits, and who will want to reorder our values and transform the heart and conscience, to make them equal to the challenge of such responsibility. What worries and oppresses us is that they might not arrive, or might go astray. Nothing is more painful than seeing an extraordinary man going astray. One who sees that man himself is degenerating, and who perceives what will be the outcome of the stupid innocence and blissful confidence of modern ideas and Christian-European morality, endures unparalleled anxiety. He sees what mankind could be and how his greatest potential is untapped. Any person who is conscious of man's overall degeneration, his reduction to a perfect herd animal (what the socialist fools call a 'free society'), and has thought through all the implications, must know no disgust but other people, and, perhaps, see a new project.

Section 6
We Scholars (pp. 93–108)

204 The harmful hierarchical shift in the relationship between science and philosophy must be opposed. One's right to speak about such a matter comes from experience, which is invariably bad. Science's declaration of independence from philosophy is one of the more subtle effects of the democratic trend. Science, having freed itself from theology, wants to be master, and legislate for philosophy. Many naive and dismissive remarks are made about philosophy, ranging from those of the utilitarian, who sees it as a succession of refuted systems, serving no useful purpose, to disdain for particular philosophers and philosophy in general. At the root of many young scholars' condescending attitude towards philosophy is the bad influence of those philosophers, who are contemptuous of their fellow philosophers' work. For example, Schopenhauer's treatment of Hegel has torn a generation of young Germans away from their relation to German culture. Again, current philosophy's impoverished state has encouraged the rabble instinct. Philosophers of the calibre of Plato are lacking. Nothing is more likely to encourage young science scholars and specialists to have a negative attitude towards philosophy than the reality philosophers or positivists. Science has a good conscience, while philosophy has sunk to the dregs. Philosophy cannot be master, when at its last gasp.

205 Today, a philosopher faces many dangers. The sheer quantity of knowledge may exhaust him, or lead him to specialize, ruling out an overview of the whole subject. If he reaches the top late, his powers will be too weak to make a worthwhile overall value judgement. He may fear becoming a dilettante, or that loss of self-respect will prevent his leading the quest for knowledge. At the same time, he knows he must make a judgement, not about the sciences, but about life and its value. He realizes that only wide-ranging experiences, perhaps disruptive and destructive ones, will equip him to do so. A popular misconception is that philosophers live prudently and apart from society, having escaped from the game of life. In fact, the true philosopher lives imprudently and continually puts himself at risk.

206 A genius is one who gives birth to things, and, compared to such a one, the average scholar is a bit of an old maid. A man of learning is industrious, moderate and conformist, desiring some independence, a place to work, and a good name. He is neither masterful nor self-sufficient, and is prone to petty envy. At his worst, his instinctive mediocrity strives to destroy the extraordinary man.

207 We are rightly sick of subjectivity, but in our desire for objectivity we must not be like the pessimists, and over-praise intellectual selflessness and depersonalization, as if ends in themselves. True, the objective person, in whom the scientific instinct is strong, is a precious tool, but he needs direction from one more powerful. The objective man is a mirror, desiring only to reflect what knowledge offers him. He neglects his own needs or suffering, through always being preoccupied with general cases. Welcoming all experiences, he is dangerously unconcerned about whether to say yes or no to life. If expected to love or hate, like God, women or animals, he does his best, but the first is often forced and the second artificial. He is genuine only if objective, and he does not know how to

deny, command or destroy. He is no model human being, for his remoteness means he has no basis on which to choose between good and evil. He is honoured too much, if seen as a philosopher, or a dictatorial breeder and tyrant of culture, as he is a slave-like being. Though valuable, he is not a goal to aim at, or one in whom the rest of existence is justified. He is neither conclusion nor beginning; neither powerful, nor autonomous, he has no wish to be master, but, like an empty vessel, awaits content, in order to take shape accordingly.

208 When a philosopher claims not to be a sceptic, no one is pleased. There is no better sedative than scepticism; sceptics do not make waves, or pose difficult choices. Like Montaigne, they prefer to wonder what they know, or, like Socrates, to say they know nothing. They think it better not to advance any hypotheses, and are beguiled by uncertainty's charms. Sceptics need comforting, as scepticism is the most spiritual expression of what might be called 'bad nerves'. It appears when long-separated races or classes suddenly intermix. The result is that everything becomes restless, doubtful and experimental, with the will in particular tending to degenerate. Even in their dreams, people doubt freedom of the will. Present-day Europe's ridiculously sudden experiment in the radical mixing of classes and races is making it thoroughly sceptical. Everywhere, there is paralysis of the will, presented as objectivity or the scientific method.

Disease of the will does not affect Europe evenly, being most severe where culture has been established longest. It is less intense where the barbarian still holds sway. The will is weakest in France, stronger in Germany, noticeably more so in England and Spain, and strongest in Russia. It may not only be wars in India and Asian entanglements that are needed to relieve Europe of its greatest danger. The increase in the Russian threat may become so great that Europe will require a new ruling caste, in order to give it a long-lived will of its own. And this will involve ending its small-state system and the multiple wills of its dynasties and democracies. By the next century, petty politics will be exchanged for politics on a grand scale; we will be fighting for mastery of the earth.

209 There is the question of the extent to which Europe's coming warlike age will foster a different, stronger sort of scepticism. That military and sceptical genius, King Frederick William I of Prussia, father of Frederick the Great, saw that Germany's deficiency was that men were lacking; and, seeing him fall prey to atheism and scepticism, feared his son might not be enough of a man. In fact, a new, manly scepticism, suited to war and conquest, was developing in Frederick. This is the German form of scepticism, which gives dangerous freedom to the spirit, but keeps the heart firmly in line. By establishing a new concept of the German spirit, with its fearlessness, tenacity and strong tendency to manly scepticism, this 'Frederickianism' has brought Europe under the German spirit's dominion. Understandably, warm-blooded and superficial people cross themselves on encountering it, but it is not long since Madame de Staël suggested that Europe should be interested in the Germans as gentle, weak-willed, poetic fools, while Napoleon was astonished that Goethe was so much a man, when he had only expected to meet a German.

210 It is debatable whether the philosophers of the future will need to be sceptics in the sense above. They will be entitled to call themselves critics, and will certainly be experimenters. In eager pursuit of knowledge, they may go further in their experiments than this soft, democratic century can allow. Undoubtedly, these new men will be the least able to give up the qualities of certainty of standards, the use of a unified method, shrewd courage, independence and self-reliance, which mark out the critic from the sceptic. They will be harsher than humane people may like, and will not engage with truth simply because they like it, or it exalts them; they will have genuine disgust for such enthusiasm, idealism and femininity. They will not intend to reconcile Christian sentiment with ancient taste or modern parliamentarianism. They will be rigorous, but will not wish to be called critics, thinking it an insult for philosophy to be regarded as merely a critical science. Although this evaluation of philosophy may have pleased even the great Kant, these new philosophers will regard critics as the philosopher's tools, and so will not be ones themselves.

211 Philosophical workers are not true philosophers. True philosophers' education may involve their going through the stages at which the former remain, and they may need to have been many things, including critic, sceptic, puzzle-solver and moralist. But these are mere preconditions for their task, which is to create values. The job of the philosophical workers, in the mould of Kant and Hegel, is to describe, clearly and intelligibly, the logical, political and aesthetic value judgements of the past. But true philosophers are commanders and lawgivers, who, using the philosophical workers' preparatory labours, reach towards the future, to lay down the way it should be. Their will to truth is the will to power. There have to be such philosophers.

212 Being, of necessity, a man of tomorrow and after, the philosopher is bound to be at odds with today. Philosophers' difficult and great task, which they cannot refuse, has been, by exposing contemporary morality's hypocrisy, smugness and falsehood, to be their age's bad conscience, and thus to mark out a new, untrodden path to human improvement.

Opposing modern ideas, which seek to limit everyone to a speciality, the philosopher must discover humanity's greatness in its breadth and variety, and in its wholeness in diversity. Today, weakness of the will is fashionable, but strength and a capacity for lengthy and difficult decisions are integral to the philosopher's idea of human greatness. In the sixteenth century, the opposite doctrine, of submissive, selfless humanity, created tidal waves of selfishness. In Socrates' day, the Athenians let themselves go for pleasure's sake, while still mouthing the same splendid words their lives had long ceased to reflect. Today's Europe honours only the herd animal, and equal rights too easily become equality of wrong, as people battle against all that is rare and privileged: the higher soul, higher duty and higher responsibility. Today, being different and living independently are integral to the concept of greatness. The philosopher proclaims that the greatest person is the one capable of being the most lonely, hidden and deviant, who is beyond good and evil, and rich in will. Greatness is being able to be multifarious and whole.

213 Learning what a philosopher is must be acquired from experience; it cannot be taught. Popular opinions about philosophy and philosophers are false, but today everybody talks about things they cannot have experienced. Few thinkers and scholars have experienced the truly philosophical coexistence of unrestrained spirituality and unerring dialectical rigour, and would consider it unbelievable. They regard thinking itself as an affliction, rather than being divine. Perhaps, artists have better insight, and know that, when they do things from necessity, feelings of freedom and creativity come into their own, and necessity and freedom of the will become one and the same. There is a hierarchy of inner states, corresponding to the hierarchy of problems, and the greatest of the latter repel those not predestined to solve them by the greatness and power of their spirituality. It is pointless for ordinary minds, or even honest craftsmen and empiricists, driven by plebeian ambition, to tackle these problems. We must be born and bred to every higher world; the primeval law of things will stop intruders entering. Our right to philosophy comes from our origins: successive generations must do the groundwork for the philosopher's development. His virtues must be cultivated, and his readiness for great responsibilities prepared. He needs to feel separated from the duties and virtues of the masses; must enjoy and practise great justice; and have the art of command and expanse of will.

Section 9 (Paragraphs 257–70)
What is Noble? (pp. 151–67)

257 Hierarchical, aristocratic societies, which valued people differently, and operated a form of slavery, were the ones that elevated human beings; and this will always be the case. Ever greater distances within the soul itself are not attainable without a sense of distance between classes, with the ruling class looking down at its underlings and tools. The truth about these higher cultures' historical origins is harsh: barbarians, whose nature was predatory, attacked weaker, peaceable races, or cultures, whose dissolution was marked by displays of wit and depravity. To start with, the barbarian caste's dominance was due to its spiritual, rather than physical strength: its members were more complete humans, and, therefore, beasts.

258 The corruption that expresses impending anarchy among the instincts, and the collapse of life's emotional foundations, varies, reflecting the form of life, in which it shows itself. It was corruption when pre-Revolutionary France's aristocracy gave up its privileges, and sacrificed itself to excessive moral feeling. This was the culmination of a process by which the aristocracy relinquished tyrannical authority, and reduced itself to a function of monarchy. In contrast, a healthy aristocracy sees itself as its society's essence, and has no qualms about oppressing incomplete people, and treating them as slaves or tools, for its own benefit. Its view is that society only exists as a means of enabling select creatures to rise to their higher task and existence.

259 Not injuring, abusing, or exploiting others makes for good manners between individuals, but should only be practised if their strengths and standards are similar, and they belong to a single social body. Making this society's basic principle would be a will to deny life, leading to decline and dissolution. Life's essence is exploitation and oppression of the foreign and weaker. To gain the upper hand, members of a healthy aristocracy do to others what they refrain from doing to each other. This is not a question of morality or immorality, but of the will to power. In Europe, people rejoice at the prospect of exploitation-free social conditions, which sounds like a life form lacking organic functions. So, far from just being a feature of primitive societies, exploitation belongs to living things' fundamental nature, deriving from the true will to power; and this is the will to life. This is a fact of all history.

260 The two basic types of moral code are master and slave moralities. In higher cultures, attempts are made to mediate between them, leading to confusion, and even to the same individual holding elements of the two. The two sources of moral value distinctions have been the master class, conscious of how it differed from the mastered, and the latter, slaves or dependants. The masters define 'good' in terms of proud, exalted states of the soul, so, in their morality, the difference

between 'good' and 'bad' is that between 'noble' and 'despicable'. There is contempt for the cowardly, the self-disparager, the craven, the flatterer and the liar.

An error of historians of morality is to start with the values that apply to actions; value distinctions are ascribed to people first. The aristocrat sees himself as determining value, so what harms him is harmful *per se*: he creates values. This is a self-glorifying moral code, with overflowing power and consciousness of wealth in the foreground. The aristocrat helps the unfortunate, but from excess of power, not pity. He relishes his own power, particularly that over himself, and respects all that is severe and harsh. Such people believe, and take pride, in themselves. They disdain empathetic feelings, and are far removed from a moral code that has pity or altruistic behaviour at its heart.

The powerful revere old age and origins, and give priority to ancestors, at the next generation's expense. If those with modern ideas have different priorities, and instinctively believe in progress and the future, this proves their views' ignoble origins. The aspect of master morality that is most at odds with current taste is that duties extend only to our peers, and that we are entitled to treat those of lower rank and foreigners as we wish: in a manner that is beyond good and evil. A noble morality is characterized by the ability and duty to be grateful or vengeful within a circle of equals; a refined concept of friendship; and a need for enemies, as outlets for envy and combativeness.

Slave morality reflects the value judgements of the oppressed, suffering and weary. Pessimistic about the human condition, they will probably condemn humanity as well. Not appreciating the virtues of the powerful, they favour moral qualities like pity, kindness and helpfulness, which will improve the lot of sufferers, or enable them to bear oppression. Slave morality is one of utility, within which the concepts of 'good' and 'evil' originated. The one who arouses fear through power and dangerousness (in master morality, the good person) is evil, while the good person is harmless and good-natured. Slave morality equates good with stupid, and emphasizes longing for freedom, while reverence and devotion characterize the aristocratic mentality.

261 The noble person cannot understand vanity: people's desire to gain others' good opinion. He will accept that he may be wrong about his own worth, but will demand that others accept his own estimate of it, or will welcome their good opinion, as he respects and loves them; it confirms his own opinion; or it is useful. Only study of history will prove to him that a common person, unaccustomed to determining values, is worth what his masters think him to be. Even today, ordinary people wait for and accept others' opinion, whether favourable or not. With the rise of democracy the noble impulse to think well of ourselves is commended, but is at odds with the older, more powerful tendency to vanity. Vain people delight in good opinions they hear about themselves, regardless of their utility or truth, instinctively accepting them. The slave is in vain people's blood, particularly women, trying to seduce them into having good opinions of themselves. It then accepts them, as if it had not invited them.

262 A species comes into being, and grows strong, through struggling against adverse conditions, but an overprotected one develops variations in type and monstrous vices. The priority of an aristocratic community, like the ancient Greek city-state, is breeding people capable of coexistence, on whom their fellow citizens can rely, and who can meet the challenges of fighting neighbours or rebellious subjects. They know the qualities that make survival possible, and these are called virtues and cultivated. In all its aspects, from the education of children to relations between the generations, the aristocratic moral code values harshness and intolerance: this is seen as a virtue, and called 'justice'. Such a species is warlike and uncommunicative.

Then, as neighbours cease to be hostile, and with material prosperity, the old discipline breaks down. At these historical turning points, there is conflict, as people are unable to accept the old moral code's restraints, but these have built up pressures within society. The point comes when the new way of life replaces the old morality. Without common standards, people must be their own lawgivers, so misunderstanding, mistrust and decline, as well as great aspirations, pour forth. Danger is the mother of morality, so there is the question of what this age's moral philosophers will preach about. They will see everything going downhill, and the incurably mediocre will be the sole survivors. Mediocrity will be the only moral code that makes sense, but it must disguise itself as proportion, duty and brotherly love.

263 Instinct for rank is the clearest sign of high rank, and joy in reverence shows noble origin. One wishing to determine the value and hierarchical position of souls will test their instinct for reverence. Continuing reverence for the Bible may be the best part of the refinement in manners that Christianity has given Europe. The protection that tyrannical external authority affords books of such depth and ultimate significance enables them to endure long enough to be explored and understood. It is a huge achievement when the masses have been trained to respect holy experiences. In contrast, the most odious characteristic of today's so-called educated people is their inability to keep their hands off anything.

There may now be more nobility among the peasants than the newspaper-reading, intellectual demi-monde.

264 It is impossible to remove the qualities and preferences of a person's ancestors from his soul. This is a problem of race: intemperance, envy, or self-righteousness, like corrupted blood, will be transmitted to the child. Upbringing or education can only deceive others about this inheritance, and, in this rabble-like age, is the purpose of both. There is no room for an educator, who teaches truthfulness, and urges his charges to be genuine and natural.

265 Egoism, the belief that others must submit to us, is in the nature of noble souls; it is in the primeval law of things. The noble soul acknowledges others with the same entitlements, and then, the issue of rank settled, relates to its equals with the modesty and reverence it shows itself. In practising this subtle self-limitation, and yielding their rights to equals, it reveres itself. Mutual reverence and rights are the essence of all society and part of the natural state of things. Mercy has no meaning between equals. Perhaps, we can be showered with gifts from above, but the noble soul is not adept in such arts, preferring to look ahead, or downwards. It knows that it is above.

266 Goethe said that the only person that can be respected is one who does not seek himself.

267 The fundamental tendency of contemporary civilizations is to make ourselves small, which would be the first thing an ancient Greek would notice.

268 For mutual understanding, there need to be common experiences, which is why a single people understand each other better than different peoples, even if they speak the same language. As they share experiences, they understand each other quickly, which is essential in times of danger. The groups of sensations, which most quickly come alive, determine the soul's values and table of goods. If necessity always brings together those who can indicate similar needs by similar signs, easy communicability of necessity must be the most powerful force controlling humans. The more similar, the more common people are. The select and rare perish in isolation. We must resist the multiplication of ordinary, average, herd-like, common people.

269 A psychologist, dealing with select cases and people, may suffocate with pity, and require a lot of cheerfulness, because souls that are different generally come to ruin. He seeks the company of ordinary people, to get away from his insights. Often, the cases he considers most pitiable are those that inspire great reverence in the crowd, which regards them as great men. The crowd loves a god, but success can lie. Their creations disguise great statesmen, conquerors and philosophers. Great poets are people of the moment, childish and frivolous, who try to escape from persistent memories in their writing, and feed on the faith their intoxicated admirers have in them. They are the targets of women's devoted pity, but, far from achieving anything, even the best love is more destructive than redemptive.

Perhaps, beneath the holy account of Jesus' life, there is one who did not receive enough human love; who invented hell as a place to send people who did not want to love him; and who then had to invent an all-loving God, who could pity paltry human love. One with that kind of knowledge of love seeks death.

270 The spiritual arrogance and loathing of one who has suffered deeply, and who, by having entered frightful worlds, knows more than most clever people, needs disguises to protect him from intrusive or pitying hands and everything that

is not equal in pain. Deep suffering ennobles, and separates, us. Such camouflages include epicureanism, which treats suffering casually; cheerfulness; being free, impertinent spirits, who conceal their shattered hearts; and folly. A more subtle humanity respects the mask, and does not pursue psychology inappropriately.

Glossary

A function of the monarchy. Part of the activity of the monarchy. The aristocracy gave up its independent authority, and became just an extension of the monarchy.

Aesthetic. That which is concerned with appreciation of beautiful objects.

Alcibiades. Fifth-century BC Athenian democratic politician and military leader, who was an important figure during the Peloponnesian War against Sparta. Admired for his talents, he was also arrogant and unreliable. He sided with Sparta for a time, and was ultimately assassinated.

Altruism. Making the welfare of others one's priority/main principle of action.

Ancient Greek *polis*. A city-state in ancient Greece, such as Athens.

Antipodal. Here that which is wholly opposed to one's own (views).

Anti-teleologists. Those who reject a teleological view of the world. See Teleological/teleology below.

Aphorism. Pithy or wise saying or maxim.

Aristophanes (c. 448–380 BC). Athenian comic poet, playwright and satirist. His plays include *The Frogs*, *The Clouds* and *The Peace*.

Aristotle (384–322 BC). Greek philosopher, student of Plato and author of such books as the *De Interpretatione*, *The Nicomachean Ethics* and *Metaphysics*.

Aristotelianism. Aristotle's moral philosophy. See Harmless mean below.

Ascetic. One who leads a life of strict self-discipline and self-denial.

Atavism. Resembling, or reverting to, distant ancestors and their (primitive) attitudes or conduct.

Atheism. The conviction that there is no God.

Athenians. Citizens of the ancient Greek city-state of Athens, noted for its learning and democratic system of government.

Glossary

Atomism/materialistic atomism. Philosophical theory, put forward by the Greek philosophers Leucippus and Democritus, that matter consists of tiny indivisible and indestructible atoms or particles, whose combinations and movements account for natural phenomena.

Atomistic need. The human need for some element that will endure, such as the soul. See also Immortal soul below.

Augustine, St (354–430). Christian philosopher and theologian, and Bishop of Hippo in North Africa. Author of *Confessions* and *The City of God*.

Bad conscience of their age. Those who oppose generally accepted, contemporary moral views.

Barbarian caste. Uncultured/uncivilized (originally, non-Greek or Roman) ruling class.

Bayle, Pierre (1647–1706). French philosopher, noted for his scepticism, whose Protestantism forced to him to leave France and live in Holland. Author of *An Historical and Critical Dictionary*.

Berkeleian or Schopenhauerian sense. The Irish philosopher, George Berkeley (Bishop of Cloyne and author of *An Essay towards a New Theory of Vision, A Treatise concerning the Principles of Human Knowledge* and *Three Dialogues between Hylas and Philonous*, 1685–1753), explained the material world in terms of (the relationship between) ideas (sensations) in the mind of the perceiver (and God). For Schopenhauer's philosophy, see I will and Schopenhauer below.

Beyond good and evil. How Nietzsche describes the 'master morality' of the 'new philosophers', which will be the antithesis of all democratic and/or Christian-based values. See Section 1, 4; Section 2, 44; Section 3, 56; Section 6, 212; Section 9, 260; and Create values and Master moralities and slave moralities below.

Borgia, Cesare (c. 1476–1507). Italian soldier and politician, and an illegitimate son of Rodrigo Borgia, Pope Alexander VI (who made him a cardinal). A successful general, he was notorious for the unscrupulous methods he used to achieve his ambitions.

Boscovich, Roger Joseph (1711–87). Physicist and professor of mathematics in Rome. Critic of the atomic theory of matter (see above), and author of *Theory of Natural Philosophy*.

Brahmans. Hindu priestly caste.

Bruno(s), Giordano (1548–1600). Italian philosopher and astrologer, who was condemned to death by the Inquisition.

Buddha or Siddhartha Gautama (c. 563–483 BC). Founder of Buddhism: 'Buddha' means 'Enlightened One'. Philosopher and teacher of noble birth, who gave up his comfortable existence for a life of poverty, contemplation and preaching.

Buddhism. Religion which teaches that life is full of suffering, as a result of the operation of karma (law of cause and effect), by which people are rewarded or punished, according to their conduct, and endure a cycle of rebirths. By following the Buddha's teaching, and overcoming their desires, they escape this cycle and achieve nirvana (extinction of desires).

Byron, George Gordon Noel, sixth Baron Byron (1788–1824). English romantic poet and dedicated supporter of Greece's independence from Turkey, whose notoriety forced him to live outside England. His works include *Childe Harold*, *Don Juan* and *Manfred*.

Caesar, Gaius Julius (c. 100–44 BC). Successful Roman general, and author of commentaries on his campaigns (*The Gallic War* and *The Civil War*), who made himself dictator of Rome, leading to his assassination.

Cagliostro, Alessandro, Conte di, or Giuseppe Balsomo (1743–95). Italian apothecary, forger and swindler, who became popular at the French court. Condemned as a heretic by the Inquisition, he died in prison.

Casual acquiescence. Agreeing with/accepting something without subjecting it to critical scrutiny.

Categorical imperative. Kant's imperative of morality, which commands unconditionally. In *Groundwork of the Metaphysics of Morals*, he maintains that what it commands must be done for its own sake, and because it is right, not to accomplish some further purpose.

Catiline, Lucius Sergius Catilina (c. 108–62 BC). Roman patrician and administrator. Defeated by Cicero in his quest for the consulship, he tried to take power by revolution and was killed in battle.

Causa sui. That one/something is the cause of him/itself.

Celts. Dominant people of central and north-western Europe during the first millennium BC. Nietzsche attributes French receptivity to, and respect for, Christianity to their 'Celtic blood'. See Section 3, 48.

Christian-ecclesiastical pressure. The influence of the Christian Church (in Europe). See Christianity below.

Christianity. Nietzsche is generally critical of Christianity, arguing that it involves sacrifice of freedom and pride, subjugation and self-derision, and is suited to the attitudes and aspirations of the slave. See Section 3, 46.

Glossary

Circulus vitiosus deus. God as a vicious circle.

Cognizance and conscience. Awareness/knowledge (of things) and awareness of what is right and wrong, which deters human beings from certain actions.

Comte, Auguste (1798–1857). French thinker and writer, founder of positivism and inventor of the term 'sociology', and author of *The System of Positive Polity*.

Contemporary morality. Generally accepted, present-day moral values, which Nietzsche attacks throughout *Beyond Good and Evil*.

Copernicus, Nicolaus (1473–1543). Polish astronomer and scientist who propounded the theory that the earth moves around the sun.

Craven. Cowardly, abject.

Create values. The new philosophers that Nietzsche longs for will not be mere academic philosophers, who study and expound past moral values, but 'commanders and lawgivers', who lay down a new set of moral values for society. See Section 6, 211.

Critical science. According to Nietzsche, philosophy's role should not just be that of a critical science: it (philosophers) must create new values, as well as subjecting existing ones to critical scrutiny. Section 6, 210.

Cromwell, Oliver (1599–1658). English landowner and member of Parliament, who became a successful cavalry general during the English Civil War. Influential in the decision to try and execute King Charles I, Cromwell governed the country (including Scotland and Ireland) as lord protector from 1653 until his death in 1658.

Cross themselves. Make the sign of the cross, to protect oneself against, or ward off, something evil.

Cynic/cynicism. Always doubting people's motives, thinking they are bad; questioning that anything is worthwhile or valuable/holding that it is not.

Da capo. From the beginning.

Darwinists. Those who accept Charles Darwin's theory of evolution, and believe that it rules out a teleological interpretation of the universe. See Teleological/teleology below.

Demi-monde. Women on the fringes of society, of questionable status and reputation.

Descartes, René (1596–1650). French rationalist philosopher and mathematician, and author of *Meditations on First Philosophy*, *Discourse on Method* and *The Principles of Philosophy*.

Glossary

Determinism. The doctrine that every event has a cause. Applied to what are held to be voluntary human actions, it suggests that they are not actually free.

Dialectic. Process of discussion and argument that enables those engaged in it to reach the truth.

Dictatorial breeder and tyrant of culture. One who creates, determines and dominates society's cultural values.

Diderot, Denis (1713–84). French philosopher, novelist and free-thinker, who along with Voltaire, Rousseau and others was an editor and major contributor to the *Encyclopédie*, which covered the various branches of learning and promoted sceptical secular views. His other works include *The Nun* and *D'Alembert's Dream*.

Dilettante. One who is an interested dabbler in a subject(s).

Dionysius. Greek god of wine, and inspirer of music and poetry.

Disinterested contemplation. In his *Critique of Judgement*, Kant explains that aesthetic judgement is disinterested: something beautiful is pleasing as an object of contemplation, not because it satisfies an appetite or desire.

Dogmatist. One who treats as true, and promotes, beliefs/views for which there is little or no evidence.

Eclectic conceptual bric-a-brac. A collection of things or ideas from a variety of sources, where the principle of selection is that they please the collector.

Egoism. Selfishness; moral system based on self-interest.

Empathetic feelings. (The desire/ability to) project oneself into/identify with someone else's personality or problems.

Empiricist/empiricism. Philosophical doctrine that (sense) experience is the (principal) source of knowledge.

Enlightenment. Term used to describe the spirit of free enquiry, rationalism and scepticism (about religious dogmas), which characterized the intellectual life of the eighteenth century, and is associated with such writers as Diderot and Voltaire.

Epicureanism. See Epicurus below.

Epicurus (341–270 BC). Greek philosopher, who settled and taught in Athens. He held that knowledge comes through the senses; that superstition should be eliminated; and that pleasure (as the only one known to the senses) is the sole good.

Epistemological scepticism. Doubt about the possibility of knowledge.

Esoteric. That which is meant for, and is only intelligible to, insiders/the initiated.

Exoteric. That which is intelligible to outsiders, the uninitiated.

Glossary

Extra-moral. Outside morality/what is moral.

Extra-sensual. Outside what can be sensed. Here, a faculty that can acquire knowledge by non-empirical means (which do not involve the senses/experience).

Faculty. Power, power of the mind.

Fatalism. Belief that events are predetermined, and will inevitably occur, whatever people do.

Father confessors. Priests in the Roman Catholic Church, to whom auricular or individual confessions of sin are made.

Foreground evaluations. Superficial, naive assessments.

Frederick II (1712–86). King of Prussia, 1740–86, and known as Frederick the Great, he was a highly successful military leader, an efficient administrator and also a patron of the arts, who expanded Prussian territory, and made Prussia into one of the leading powers in Europe.

Frederick the Great. See Frederick II above.

Frederick William I (1688–1740). King of Prussia, 1713–40, who developed Prussia's administration and economy, and turned it into a major European power. He was the father of Frederick the Great, with whom he was often on bad terms.

Frederickianism. Nietzsche's term for what he describes as the 'daring, manly scepticism' of Frederick the Great, which was suited to 'war and conquest'. See Section 6, 209.

Free will/freedom of the will. The doctrine that the human will is free, and that people can be held responsible for what they do and rightly punished if they do wrong.

Freethinking/thinkers. Speculating/those who speculate freely about the existence of God and religious issues.

French Revolution. The Revolution in France, which started with the storming of the Bastille in 1789, and led to the overthrow of the French monarchy and the execution of Louis XVI. Nietzsche describes it as 'gruesome' and a 'superfluous farce', on to which commentators project their own interpretations and views. See Section 2, 38.

God on the Cross. Jesus Christ, whom Christians believe is the Son of God, was crucified by the Romans.

Goethe, Johann Wolfgang von (1749–1832). Influential German novelist, poet and thinker, whose works include *Faust*, *Hermann and Dorothea* and *Wilhelm Meister*.

Gogol, Nikolai Vasilyevich (1809–52). Russian novelist and playwright, whose works include *The Government Inspector* and *Mirgorod*.

Glossary

Grand feeling of distance between classes. Clear distinctions/separation between the various classes that make up society.

Greatest number. Utilitarians hold that right actions are those that maximize the happiness of the greatest number of people.

Harmful per se. Harmful in itself.

Harmless mean. In his *The Nicomachean Ethics*, Aristotle puts forward the doctrine of the mean: that virtue is finding the mean or mid point between the vices of excess and deficiency. According to Nietzsche, this tones down the passions, and blunts the will to power. See Section 5, 198.

Hegel, Georg Wilhelm Friedrich (1770–1831). German philosopher, professor of philosophy at Berlin, and author of such works as *The Phenomenology of Mind* and *The Philosophy of Right*, whose ideas had a major impact on the course of philosophy in the nineteenth century.

Hellenic culture. The culture of Ancient Greece.

Heraclites (of Ephesus). Fifth-century Greek philosopher, who taught that matter derives from fire, and that the world is in a constant state of flux or change.

Hierarchical shift. A reversal in the relative importance (of science and philosophy).

Historical turning points. Points in history when major changes occur.

Homines religiosi. Religious men.

Human aggrandizement. An increase in human power/greatness.

I think. In his search for something absolutely certain, which will provide a secure base for all knowledge, Descartes finds there is one thing that he cannot doubt: that he is a thinking thing ('I think, therefore I am': *Discourse on Method*).

I will. Schopenhauer (*The World as Will and Idea*), following Kant's distinction between the noumenal world (things as they are in themselves) and the phenomenal world (the world as it appears to us), identifies the will with 'the thing in itself', which stands outside space and time, and to which everything else is subordinate.

Immortal soul. In Plato, the indestructible spiritual element, which is reborn after a period in heaven or the underground world; in Christianity, the seat of personality and individual identity, which lives on after death, and which will be reunited with its body at the general resurrection.

Ineradicable, eternal, indivisible, a monad, an atom. The nature of the soul, which is indestructible, endures for ever and (unlike the body) is incapable of being divided (and so is immortal). See also Atomism above and Monad below.

Instinctual activity. Something done from instinct, spontaneous.

Intellectual intuition. Immediate mental awareness/apprehension.

Intelligible character. That which can be discovered/known about by the mind/ intellect. See Theory of the forms below.

Inter pares. Among equals.

Ipseity. Concern with/emphasis on the self.

Ironic. Giving what is said additional force by using words with a literal meaning that is the opposite of what is meant.

Irrational aspect of moral judgements. That moral judgements are not always/wholly determined by reason, but by the instincts/ emotions.

Jesuitism/Jesuitical. Related to/connected with the Jesuits (Society of Jesus), the religious order started by Ignatius Loyola in the sixteenth century, which by emphasizing obedience and loyalty to the Pope aimed to reinvigorate the Roman Catholic Church, through missionary and educational work. The term 'Jesuitical' is used in a derogatory sense, to indicate one who dissembles or equivocates to obtain the best outcome.

Jesus (Christ) (c. 5/6 BC–c. 30 AD). Founder of Christianity, whose life of preaching and healing is described in the New Testament, and whom Christians believe to be the incarnate Word of God and the second person of the Trinity.

Kant, Immanuel (1724–1804). Influential German philosopher, whose writings cover metaphysics, moral philosophy and philosophy of religion, and include *Critique of Pure Reason, Critique of Practical Reason, Religion within the Boundaries of Mere Reason* and *Groundwork of the Metaphysics of Morals*.

Kundry. A character in Richard Wagner's opera, *Parsifal*.

Laisser-aller. Letting things go, non-interference.

Leonardo da Vinci (1452–1519). Florentine painter, sculptor and scientist, whose works include 'Mona Lisa', 'The Last Supper' and 'The Adoration of the Magi'.

Lessing, Gotthold Ephraim (1729–81). German dramatist and literary critic, whose works include *Miss Sara Sampson, The Disbanded Officer* and *Emilia Galotti* (plays), and *Laocoon*.

Locke, John (1632–1704). British empiricist philosopher, medical practitioner and government administrator, whose books include *An Essay Concerning Human Understanding, Two Treatises of Government* and *The Reasonableness of Christianity*.

Glossary

Logic. Science of inference or reasoning.

Luther, Martin (1483–1546). German theologian and one-time Augustinian friar, whose protest in 1517 against the sale of papal indulgences (intended to remit the penance for confessed and absolved sinners, but popularly believed to shorten the times souls – including those of the dead – would spend in purgatory) in Germany, led to a wider attack on Roman Catholic doctrines and practices, resulting in the Reformation and the establishment of Protestant Churches in Europe.

Machiavelli, Niccolò (1469–1527). Florentine political philosopher, historian and government administrator. His best-known work, *The Prince*, argues that to ensure success and the security of their states rulers must not be bound by accepted moral rules (as Cesare Borgia had exemplified).

Madame de Staël, Germaine, Baronne de Staël-Holstein (1766–1817). French writer, famous for her international literary salon and for promoting the cause of female writers. Her books include *Delphine* and *Corinne, or Italy* (novels) and *Germany*.

Master moralities and slave moralities. Nietzsche explains the difference between 'master morality', which associates what is good with power, pride and nobility and disdains empathetic feelings, and 'slave morality', which values pity, kindness and helpfulness, the qualities most likely to improve the lot of the slave or sufferers, in Section 9, 260.

Metaphysician/metaphysics. One who studies/the study of what is after (beyond) physics, and which cannot be investigated by ordinary empirical methods; the investigation of what really exists, of ultimate reality.

Monad. An idea propounded by the German philosopher Leibniz (Baron Gottfried Wilhelm von Leibniz, 1646–1716, whose works include *Discourse of Metaphysics, Theodicy* and *Monadology*) that God has so designed the universe that it consists ultimately of conscious and volitional entities, or monads, which develop and operate independently of each other.

Montaigne, Michel Eyquem de (1533–92). French philosopher and essayist, noted for his philosophical scepticism and his *Essays*.

Moral faculty. A faculty for apprehending what is good or bad, right or wrong. In his *Groundwork of the Metaphysics of Morals*, Kant argues that *a priori* (that which comes before experience) moral principles (the moral law), which should govern the actions of all rational beings, are discovered by the reason.

Glossary

Morphology and evolutionary theory of the will to power. The form and development of the will to power.

Multifarious and whole. To be one person with many dimensions or facets.

Multiple wills of its dynasties and democracies. The varying aims of the monarchies and democratic governments that rule the different European states.

Napoleon (Bonaparte) (1769–1821). Corsican-born soldier, who became Emperor of France in 1804, and conquered a large part of Europe before his final defeat at Waterloo and exile to St Helena.

Nets of concepts. See Intelligible character above.

New breed of philosophers. See Create values above.

New philosophers. See Create values above.

Nihilism. Belief that there is nothing in life to believe in or value; rejection of all religious/moral beliefs and values.

Old god. Belief in God, traditional religious/Christian beliefs.

Origin of ideas. In his *Essay Concerning Human Understanding*, Locke argues that words prevent us gaining access to things in themselves, as they only stand for ideas.

Paradox/paradoxical. Statement/something that appears, but may not be, absurd or self-contradictory.

Pascal, Blaise (1623–62). French mathematician, scientist, philosopher and theologian, whose works include his *Pensées*.

Penitence. Feeling sorrow or regret (for sin).

Perspectivity/perspectivist. Seeing/one who sees things/issues, or believes they can be seen, from more than one point of view.

Petronius (Arbiter), Gaius (died AD 65). Roman consul and governor, satirical writer.

Philology/philologist. Study of/one who studies (the development of) languages.

Philosopher. One who studies and practises/teaches philosophy, the study of ultimate reality, what really exists, the most general principles of things.

Philosophical idealist. Philosopher who holds that reality is, in some sense, mental/in the mind.

Philosophical workers. The academic philosophers, who prepare the ground for the new philosophers. See Create values above and Section 6, 211.

Philosophy of Vedanta. One of the six orthodox schools of Hindu philosophy, which bases its doctrines on the final part of the Veda (collections of Hindu teachings), the Upanishads. One strand of interpretation within Vedanta is that the soul or self is distinct from Brahman (the Absolute).

Phlegm. Slow to feel or show emotion(s).

Physiological imperative. What is decreed by the way living things normally function.

Physiologist. One who studies living things' normal functions.

Physio-psychology. A study of how human beings function physically and mentally.

Plato (C. 429–C. 347 BC). Greek philosopher and pupil of Socrates, who founded the Academy (the world's first university) in Athens, where Aristotle studied, and whose many writings include *The Republic*, *Theaetetus*, *Symposium*, *Phaedrus* and *Laws*.

Platonic method. See Intelligible character above.

Platonism for the common people. Nietzsche's description of Christianity. See Christianity above.

Plebeian ambition. The ambition of the common people, the lowest classes in society.

Poe, Edgar Allan (1809–49). American poet, short-story writer and literary critic, whose works include *Tales of Mystery and Imagination*.

Positivism/positivist. A form of empiricism developed by Comte, which holds that sense experience is the only or best type of knowledge, as it does not involve speculation.

Preordained. Determined beforehand.

Primordial law of things. The original, primitive law of things.

Protestant (Christianity). Nietzsche makes the point (Section 3, 48) that Roman Catholicism is more deeply rooted among southern Europeans than Protestantism is among northern Europeans, who thus find it easier to shake off religious beliefs and the constraints they impose. See also Luther above.

Pure spirit. See Immortal soul above.

Puritanism. Here a strictly self-disciplined and self-denying religious way of life.

Rabble of the senses. The varied, ever-changing and confusing information that comes to us through our senses. See also Intelligible character above.

Rationalism. Philosophical doctrine that reason, rather than (sense) experience, is the (principal) source of knowledge.

Reality-philosophists. See Positivism/positivist above.

Reality philosophers. See Positivism/positivist above.

Real-political. A reference to 'realpolitik' or 'practical politics', which is particularly associated with Bismarck (Prince Otto Edward

Glossary

Leopold von, 1815–98), who as prime minister of Prussia used a combination of war and adroit diplomacy to secure the unification of Germany under Prussia's leadership, and became its first Chancellor.

Reciprocal conditionality. Being mutually dependent conditions of each other.

Reductio ad absurdum. Reducing an argument to absurdity by finding a contradiction in the assumptions on which it is based, such that one or more has to be abandoned.

Religious neurosis. Religious disorder.

Renan, Joseph Ernest (1823–92). French religious historian and author of *History of the Origins of Christianity* and *History of the People of Israel*.

Rococo of sensibility. Elaborately ornate expression of (a capacity for) emotions/sensitivities. This is Nietzsche's description of the New Testament, whose emphasis on compassion and mercy he compares unfavourably to the more robust religious outlook found in the Old Testament (Section 3, 52).

Russian nihilism. Reference to views of Russian revolutionaries, committed to the overthrow of the existing order.

Sabbath of Sabbaths. From Augustine, *City of God*, Book XXII.

Saint(e)-Beuve, Charles Augustin (1804–69). French literary critic and writer, and author of *A History of Port-Royal*.

Salvation Army. Founded by William Booth in 1865, and dedicated to Christian mission and helping those in need. Nietzsche regards its evangelical fervour as another manifestation of the religious neurosis (Section 3, 47).

Satyr. Lustful individual, full of sexual desires.

Sceptical anti-realists. Philosophers opposed to positivism/extreme forms of empiricism. See also Idealism and Rationalism above.

Scepticism. Generally, doubt, or refusing to accept non-empirical sources of knowledge. See also Epistemological scepticism above.

Schelling, Friedrich Wilhelm Joseph von (1775–1854). German idealist philosopher and author of *The Philosophy of Art*.

Schopenhauer, Arthur (1788–1860). German philosopher, author of *The World as Will and Idea* and opponent of Hegel's idealism, who was noted for his emphasis on pessimism and despair, and his interest in Buddhism, which influenced his philosophical views. Nietzsche is very critical of Schopenhauer's ideas. See Section 1, 16, 19; Section 3, 47, 56; Section 5, 186; Section 6, 204. See also I will and Buddhism above.

Glossary

Science's Declaration of Independence from philosophy. Scientific investigation was initially a branch of philosophy.

Self-disparager. One who is self-critical, self-diminishing.

Sensualism. Preoccupation with, being dedicated to, the pleasures of the senses (as opposed to the intellect).

Shaw, George Bernard (1856–1950). Irish playwright and novelist, whose thinking was influenced by Nietzsche's ideas. His plays include *Man and Superman*, *Major Barbara* and *Pygmalion*.

Sin. Offence against/disobeying, God.

Small-state system. Europe's consisting of a number of (relatively) small, independent states.

Socialistic compassion. Feeling(s) of pity (for the poor), reflecting/ deriving from belief in human equality and the need for common/ state ownership of assets.

Socrates (c. 470–399 BC). Athenian philosopher, who devoted his life to pursuit of philosophical truth, but who was executed for undermining belief in the gods and corrupting youth.

Socratism. Nietzsche's term for the view Plato associates with Socrates, in some of his dialogues, that people do bad things because they do not know they are bad.

Spinoza, Benedictus or Baruch de (1632–77). Dutch rationalist philosopher and lens-maker, whose works include *Tractatus Theologico-Politicus* and *Ethics*.

Spinoza's inconsistency. See Spinoza, *Ethics* (Part IV, Proposition XX), where he argues that it is impossible that a human being should seek to become non-existent from the necessity of his own nature, as opposed to external causes.

Stendhal (1788–1842). The pseudonym of the French writer and literary critic Henri Beyle, whose books include *The Red and the Black* and *The Charterhouse of Parma*.

Stoics. School of Greek philosophy, which taught self-control and un-complaining fortitude in the face of pain and adversity.

Substance. The essence of something, which makes it what it is. Many metaphysicians held that the universe consists of one (or more) fundamental substance(s).

Super-Asiatic eye. Greater than, or above, an Asiatic outlook: Nietzsche is referring to Schopenhauer's interest in Buddhism.

Supreme divinatory refinement of the historical sense. A reference to Hegel's view that despite evidence to the contrary history can be interpreted as human beings' progress towards self-consciousness of spirit.

Glossary

Synthesis. Something that is built up from separate elements.

Synthetic a priori (judgements). Judgements in which the concept of the subject does not contain the concept of the predicate, so the predicate adds something to the subject, but which are known *a priori* (independently of experience) to be certainly true.

Synthetic concept 'I'. According to Nietzsche, the separate acts of commanding and obeying become fused together as 'willing', and subsumed under the idea of the 'I' or self, such that they cease to be distinct (Section 1, 19).

Table of categories. The general categories of thought, such as unity, causality, existence, and so on. In his *Critique of Pure Reason*, Kant divides them into four groups: (of) quantity, quality, relation and modality.

Table of goods. The (relative order) of the things a person considers good (or bad).

Taciturn. Inclined not to speak, preferring silence.

Taxonomy of morals. A classification of moral principles.

Teleological/teleology. The view that things in the world, particularly human beings, have an end or purpose, which they do/ought to aim at. This may be due to their nature or to their being directed by God.

The ideal of the Good. See Theory of the forms and Transcendental goodness below.

The text has disappeared underneath the interpretation. There is so much interpretation (of the French Revolution) that it is impossible to determine the events or their causes.

Theism. Belief in God.

Theology/theologian. Setting out the beliefs and teachings of a religion in a systematic way; academic discipline concerned with study of religion/religious beliefs and teachings; (theologian) one who studies/teaches theology.

Theory of the forms. Plato held that individual things in the ordinary, visible world, which we experience through our senses, acquire their identity by being (in some sense) copies of the unchanging forms of these things in the intelligible world, to which only our minds can give us access. Thus, something is round by being a copy of, or participating in, the form of roundness. However, it will not be perfectly round, but will only approximate to roundness. See also Transcendental goodness below.

Thing in itself/things in themselves. Things as they are in themselves

Glossary

(what Kant called the noumenal world), as opposed to how they appear to us (phenomenal world).

Titles of his major works. A reference to the titles of some of Kant's major works: *Critique of Pure Reason*, *Critique of Practical Reason* and *Critique of Judgement*.

Touchstone. Standard/criterion for judging something.

Transcendental goodness. Plato held that the form of the good has the same relation to intelligible objects in the intelligible world as the sun has to visible objects in the visible world, and is the source of reality, truth and goodness. See also Theory of the forms above.

Truly philosophical coexistence of unrestrained spirituality and unerring dialectical rigour. Nietzsche is describing what he regards as the nature of true philosophical enquiry, which he believes few scholars have experienced: that engaging in rigorous philosophical investigation and argument is spiritually uplifting (Section 6, 213).

Tubingen Stift. A reference to the Faculty of Theology at the University of Tubingen in Germany.

Unidirectional. Direction/government by one person or body.

Utilitarianism/utilitarian. Consequentialist moral systems (ones that decide whether an action is right or wrong on the basis of its consequences), which hold that actions are not right or wrong in themselves, but only to the extent to which they promote pleasure/happiness and prevent pain.

Utility. Usefulness. See Utilitarianism above.

Venice. Under aristocratic government, the Republic of Venice became a powerful state and Europe's major sea-power during the fourteenth and fifteenth centuries.

Virtue. Moral excellence, a positive character trait that makes someone morally good and admirable.

Voltaire, François-Marie Arouet (1694–1778). French poet, dramatist and philosopher. Noted for his attacks on religion and author of *Essays on the Manners and Spirit of Nations* and *Candide, or All for the Best*.

Voluptuousness. Indulgence in things that provide luxury and pleasure.

Wagner, Richard (1813–83). German composer and conductor, whose major operatic works include *Lohengrin*, *Tannhäuser* and *The Ring*.

Wholeness in diversity. That the philosopher will become well-rounded intellectually, and best able to pursue his investigations, not by specializing in one area but by exposing himself to a range of subjects.

Will to power. Nietzsche describes it (Section 5, 186 and 2, 36) as the 'essence' of the world, such that 'all our organic functions' could be explained as the 'development' of this one 'basic form of the will'.

Will to truth. Philosophers' determination to discover the truth.